Old Testament
Textual Criticism

Old Testament
Textual Criticism
A Practical Introduction

Ellis R. Brotzman

Foreword by Bruce K. Waltke

Baker Books
A Division of Baker Book House Co
Grand Rapids, Michigan 49516

Published by Baker Books
a division of Baker Book House Company
P.O. Box 6287, Grand Rapids, MI 49516-6287

Sixth printing, Febuary 2002

Printed in the United States of America

Library of Congress Cataloging-in-Publication Data

Brotzman, Ellis R.
    Old Testament textual criticism : a practical introduction / Ellis
R. Brotzman ; foreword by Bruce K. Waltke.
        p.   cm.
    Includes bibliographical references and index.
    ISBN 0-8010-1065-9
    1. Bible. O.T.—Criticism, Textual. I. Title.
BS1136.B765   1994
221.4′4—dc20   93-42726

For information about academic books, resources for Christian leaders,
and all new releases available from Baker Book House, visit our web site:
http://www.bakerbooks.com/

For Ruth
Like her biblical namesake,
she too is אֵשֶׁת חַיִל
(a capable woman)

Contents

Foreword

Bruce K. Waltke

Until recently there was no suitable textbook for the discipline of Old Testament textual criticism. The standard work by Bleddyn J. Roberts, *The Old Testament Text and Versions*, had become out of date.[1] But now two excellent texts have appeared: Emanuel Tov's *Textual Criticism of the Hebrew Bible* and this one by Ellis Brotzman.[2]

Unfortunately, on the one hand, Brotzman did not have Tov's work available to him when preparing his manuscript (this deficiency was corrected before going to press). I had prepublication access to Tov's work and some of its material was mediated to Brotzman through my essay "Old Testament Textual Criticism" in the forthcoming *Holman Introduction to the Bible*, edited by David S. Dockery, Kenneth A. Mathews, and Robert Sloan (Nashville: Broadman). Fortunately, on the other hand, Tov's and Brotzman's books complement each other. Brotzman takes time to present the contribution of the ancient versions, but Tov deliberately slights them. Tov devotes an entire chapter to textual criticism and literary criticism, especially in the light of the five (not three) recensions attested among the Dead Sea Scrolls, but Brotzman in his discussion of the significance of the Dead Sea Scrolls does not elaborate on this contribution to our understanding of the development of the Old Testament.

1. Published in 1951 by the University of Wales Press, Cardiff.
2. Tov's book was published by Fortress Press in 1992.

Brotzman makes a unique contribution in his discussion of textual criticism and inspiration. In that connection, Douglas Stuart makes the significant observation: "It is fair to say that the verses, chapters, and books of the Bible would read largely the same, and would leave the same impressions with the reader, even if one adopted virtually every possible *alternative* reading to those now serving as the basis for current English translations."[3]

Actually, the variety of text types attested in the Dead Sea Scrolls underscores that their relatively large consensus is due to their close genetic relation to the original, not to collusion. Shemaryahu Talmon notes:

> The scope of variation within all these textual traditions is relatively restricted. Major divergencies which intrinsically affect the sense are extremely rare. A collation of variants extant, based on the synoptic study of the material available, either by a comparison of parallel passages within one Version, or of the major Versions with each other, results in the conclusion that the ancient authors, compilers, tradents and scribes enjoyed what may be termed a controlled freedom of textual variation.[4]

Laird Harris provides this apt analogue from science for the reliability of the text, in spite of no perfect witnesses to it. He observes that loss or destruction of the standard yard at the Smithsonian Institution would not enormously affect the practice of measurements in the United States, for a comparison of the multitudinous copies of that yard would lead us to something very close to the original standard.[5]

3. Douglas Stuart, "Inerrancy and Textual Criticism," in *Inerrancy and Common Sense*, ed. Roger R. Nicole and J. Ramsey Michaels (Grand Rapids: Baker, 1980), 98.

4. Shemaryahu Talmon, "The Textual Study of the Bible—A New Outlook," in *Qumran and the History of the Biblical Text*, ed. Frank M. Cross and Shemaryahu Talmon (Cambridge: Harvard University Press, 1975), 326.

5. R. Laird Harris, *Inspiration and Canonicity of the Bible* (Grand Rapids: Zondervan, 1957), 88–89.

Figures

Tables

Abbreviations

ABD	David N. Freedman et al. (eds.), *The Anchor Bible Dictionary* (6 vols.; New York: Doubleday, 1992)
BDB	Francis Brown, Samuel R. Driver, and Charles A. Briggs, *A Hebrew and English Lexicon of the Old Testament* (Oxford: Clarendon, 1907; corrected printing in 1953)
BHK	Rudolf Kittel (ed.), *Biblia Hebraica* (3d ed.; Stuttgart: Württembergische Bibelanstalt, 1937)
BHS	Karl Elliger and Wilhelm Rudolph (eds.), *Biblia Hebraica Stuttgartensia* (Stuttgart: Deutsche Bibelgesellschaft, 1977)
GKC	Emil Kautzsch (ed.), *Gesenius' Hebrew Grammar* (trans. Arthur E. Cowley; 2d ed.; Oxford: Clarendon, 1910)
LXX	Septuagint
MT	Masoretic Text
SP	Samaritan Pentateuch

Introduction

Old Testament textual criticism is viewed by most beginning students as a very complicated matter. The antipathy felt by many potential exegetes toward basic study of the Hebrew language is only magnified when they are introduced to the study of Old Testament textual criticism. This book is written with those bewildered students in mind. It aims to help them understand the textual transmission of the Hebrew text and, even more, to actually involve them in the critical study of the Old Testament text.

Need for Old Testament Textual Criticism

Two extreme views exist regarding the need for textual criticism of the Old Testament.[1] The first holds that the Hebrew text has been so carefully transmitted that textual criticism is, for all practical purposes, unnecessary. The second maintains that the text of the Old Testament is so uncertain that it is impossible for text critics to recover the original form of the Hebrew Scriptures.

As a first step, it must be recognized that the textual situations are quite different for the two Testaments. The New Testament text is attested by a very large number of Greek manuscripts, some very old, and they all reflect a large number of

1. These extremes are more appropriately opposing tendencies, but they are described as extremes in order to make the contrast between them more noticeable.

variant readings. The Old Testament text, in contrast, is supported by far fewer, but generally better, Hebrew manuscripts. Students of the Old Testament text thus have to deal with fewer variants than their New Testament counterparts.[2] The preceding description of the general character of textual criticism in the two Testaments has a historical basis. It is generally accepted that the Old Testament was copied more carefully than the New. But does careful copying mean a total absence of variant readings? Is a carefully copied text necessarily a perfect text? The answer to both questions is no. The earliest books of the Old Testament were copied by hand for some three thousand years before they were first produced in printed form. Moreover, the earliest forms of the Old Testament text were written in an exclusively consonantal form. While word division was surely indicated in early manuscripts, occasional crowding apparently led to errors in the division between words.[3] Certain consonants were added in an intermediate stage to indicate many final vowels and at a later stage to represent some medial vowels. The complete system of vowel notation, as distinct from the consonantal text, was only written down at a later stage (between A.D. 600 and 1000).

These brief references to the early history of the Old Testament text indicate the potential for the introduction of variant readings that the beginning exegete needs to deal with knowledgeably.[4] The ability to make text-critical judgments

2. James Barr, *Comparative Philology and the Text of the Old Testament* (reprinted Winona Lake, Ind.: Eisenbrauns, 1987), 4, notes that in the case of a "non-uniform text" (the situation of the New Testament) textual criticism focuses on a discussion of variant readings. With a "uniform text" (the situation of the Old Testament), however, textual criticism tends to focus on problem passages. See also Norman L. Geisler and William E. Nix, *A General Introduction to the Bible*, rev. ed. (Chicago: Moody, 1986), 465–67.

3. The issue of word division versus continuous writing in early Hebrew manuscripts is disputed. The older consensus held that early manuscripts were written continuously, i.e., without word division indicated. Recent studies, however, have shown that this earlier consensus was mistaken. Further details may be found in chapter 2.

4. The Old Testament student needs such knowledge if only to evaluate the text-critical decisions found in modern English translations, critical commentaries, and technical journal articles.

is developed through awareness of the history of the transmission of the Old Testament text.

While some downplay the need for Old Testament textual criticism, others emphasize it to such an extent that the basic trustworthiness of the text is placed in doubt. Shemaryahu Talmon has written the following with regard to the Old Testament text:

> The scholar who takes a synoptic view of all the sources at his disposal is confronted with a bewildering plethora of *variae lectiones* in the extant versions of the Old Testament books. . . . It should be borne in mind that the printed editions represent the end of a long chain of textual development and of editorial activities which were aimed at unifying the sacred texts. These late editions can in no way be taken to exhibit faithfully the autographs of the biblical authors. In fact not one single verse of this ancient literature has come to us in an original manuscript, written by a biblical author or by a contemporary of his, or even by a scribe who lived immediately after the time of the author. . . . Even a cursory perusal of the sources available immediately reveals that not one tradition and not one manuscript is without fault.[5]

To be sure, Talmon quickly balances this statement by saying that "these errors and textual divergences between the versions materially affect the intrinsic message only in relatively few instances."[6] Yet his first statement is illustrative of the extreme to which an overemphasis on textual variants can lead.

The position this book seeks to establish is that both extremes should be avoided. It is evident that some errors have crept into the text during its long transmission. It would be naïve to dismiss any textual corruption out of hand. Obviously, these errors must be discovered and corrected. But the Old Testament student must also realize that the Hebrew text has been transmitted with great care. Errors will be found in the study of the text, but they are not so numerous or so crucial that they destroy its basic credibility.

5. Shemaryahu Talmon, "The Old Testament Text," in *The Cambridge History of the Bible*, vol. 1: *From the Beginnings to Jerome*, ed. Peter R. Ackroyd and Christopher F. Evans (Cambridge: Cambridge University Press, 1970), 161–62.
6. Ibid., 162.

Elements of Old Testament Textual Criticism

What then are the activities involved in actually performing textual criticism of the Old Testament? What must the beginning Old Testament text critic be able to do? First, the text critic must be aware of at least the basics of the history of the transmission of the Old Testament text. This includes both the Hebrew text and the ancient versions of the Old Testament. An awareness of how scribes copied—and of how translators rendered—the text will help the student text critic deal with variant readings. Second, the text critic must seek to determine[7] which of the variant readings for a given text is the most acceptable.[8]

But what does "most acceptable" mean?[9] At an earlier stage in the history of Old Testament textual criticism, the aim of the discipline was to discover the original wording of the text as it left the hand of the inspired author. Subsequent text critics have described the aim of textual criticism as discovering the final form of the text, or the earliest attested text, or the text accepted by a particular religious group. Recently there has even been an awareness of the existence of more than a single form of a given text.[10] At this point in the discussion, the second task

7. The word *determine* implies that the original wording can be found in at least one of the Hebrew or versional witnesses to the Old Testament text. In some cases it may be that no ancient witness contains the original wording, and in such cases the text critic must resort to conjectural emendation to restore the text. The field of Old Testament text criticism is divided on both the advisability of conjectural emendation and the extent to which it can or should be used. For further details, see chapter 7.

8. See, e.g., Talmon, "Old Testament Text," 163, who speaks of these two broad areas of the text critic's work.

9. The discussion that follows is heavily indebted to Bruce K. Waltke, "Aims of OT Textual Criticism," *Westminster Theological Journal* 51 (1989): 93–108.

10. Ibid., 102–7. Waltke cites the existence of various parallel texts in the Old Testament and suggests that the text critic in these cases should accept both forms of the text rather than try to press behind the two (or more) forms to a supposed more original form. More recently Waltke, following Tov, argues that for certain Old Testament books there was more than a single edition published; this holds true especially for Jeremiah and Ezekiel. See Bruce K. Waltke, "Old Testament Textual Criticism," in *Holman Introduction to the Bible*, ed. David S. Dockery, Kenneth A. Mathews, and Robert Sloan (Nashville: Broadman, forthcoming).

of the text critic will be simply expressed as the attempt to discover the "best" text (the nuances of which will be clarified in chapter 7). The determination of the best wording of the text must be based, insofar as is possible, on principles that are consistent with ancient scribal practices.

Plan of Attack

Following the introduction, chapter 1 deals with writing in the ancient Near East. Why, the reader may ask, is it necessary in a book on Old Testament textual criticism to speak of the history of writing in antiquity? It is necessary—and desirable—because a general understanding of ancient writing practices allows a better understanding of the transmission of the text of the Hebrew Bible and of how its best wording may be determined.

The next three chapters cover the transmission of the Old Testament text. Chapter 2 traces the history of the transmission of the text in Hebrew from the time of the writing of the individual biblical books until our modern era. Chapter 3 summarizes the most important aspects of the transmission of the Old Testament text by means of the ancient versions. Though not strictly a version, the Samaritan Pentateuch is also included in chapter 3. Chapter 4 serves as an introduction to the Dead Sea Scrolls. Though these early documents form a part of the history of the transmission of the Old Testament text, it is helpful to deal with them in their own right because of their relatively recent discovery and importance to the field of text criticism.

Given the information about the transmission of the text, how do we discover what is the best reading in a particular verse of the Old Testament? Chapters 5–8 describe the practical steps involved in determining the most original reading. Chapter 5 introduces the critical apparatus and layout of *Biblia Hebraica Stuttgartensia* (*BHS*). I am well aware of the dangers inherent in seeking to perform textual criticism solely on the basis of *BHS*.[11]

11. Critics of *BHS* usually emphasize that the information listed is incomplete and that some of what is listed is incorrect. See James Barr, "Review of *Biblia Hebraica Stuttgartensia*," *Journal of Semitic Studies* 25 (1980): 98–105; Ralph W. Klein, *Textual Criticism of the Old Testament* (Philadelphia: Fortress, 1974), 62–63, cites Harry M. Orlinsky's analogous criticism of *BHK*.

Yet is it not obvious that the beginning text critic needs to start at just this point? For that reason this book will focus on this preliminary—but also necessary—stage of textual criticism, that is, making use of the information included in *BHS*.

Chapter 6 surveys the typical kinds of scribal errors—both inadvertent and intentional—that have been introduced into the Old Testament text through the years. Chapter 7 focuses on the principles for establishing the best text. These principles include how to evaluate both external and internal evidence. In a new emphasis among books on textual criticism, chapter 8 presents a textual commentary on the Book of Ruth. It seems clear that an extended treatment of the textual issues in a short Old Testament book will offer a decided advantage over the more usual discussion of various independent textual problems scattered throughout the Old Testament.

The conclusion summarizes the results of this study of textual criticism. It prepares the student to continue critical study of the Old Testament text. In addition, the final chapter indicates what steps are needed for the reader to pursue advanced textual analysis of the Hebrew Bible.

Textual Criticism and Inspiration

A final word is in order before beginning. Textual criticism is sometimes viewed as somehow opposed to the traditional teaching about the inspiration and authority of the Old Testament. Most evangelical statements on the inspiration of Scripture refer in some way to the autographs. Yet for many this amounts to a hollow statement, since no one today has direct access to any of the autographs of Scripture.[12]

It seems obvious, given the nature of the transmission of the text of Scripture, that none of our current texts or versions is identical to the autographs. Douglas Stuart states: "The problems are real. There is no chapter of the Bible for which

---

12. Compare the statements of faith of the several evangelical seminaries or of evangelical church bodies. These two qualifications (the locus of the inspired text and the unavailability of the autographs) are equally applicable to the text of either Testament.

all ancient manuscripts have exactly the same wording. Many chapters, in fact, display textual problems in virtually every verse."[13] Thus it is evident that scribal errors have found their way into the ancient manuscripts and modern versions of both Testaments. Given this, it seems only proper to define inspiration in terms of the autographs.

There is a second issue, however. What about the charge that describing inspiration in relation to the autographs is a hollow or meaningless statement? It is important to deal with this issue directly at the outset of this work. As Bruce Waltke points out, it is important to set the issue in perspective. He suggests that, on average, there is about one textual note in *BHS* for each ten words. Textual criticism, by its very nature, focuses on the variant readings, but the 90% or more of the text that exists without variation must also be kept in view.[14] In addition, Gleason L. Archer Jr. outlines the difference between nonauthoritative autographs and inspired, though not directly available, autographs. If we had to deal with autographs of doubtful authority, we would need more than our finite knowledge to decide what is truth and what is error. This is not the case, however, with inspired though not accessible autographs. Humans are capable of discovering errors in the transmission of a text.[15] Roger R. Nicole observes that "a slip in the transcriptional process is always subject to human correction. This is an area in which men are competent to act and to express meaningful opinions."[16] Perhaps a modern-day example will help. A letter or a newspaper article that contains a few typographical errors, but is written by an honest person, is obviously of great value to the reader. The errors can be identified and corrected, and the message received can be trusted. Such is not the case with a letter or

---

13. Douglas Stuart, "Inerrancy and Textual Criticism," in *Inerrancy and Common Sense*, ed. Roger R. Nicole and J. Ramsey Michaels (Grand Rapids: Baker, 1980), 98.
14. Waltke, "Old Testament Textual Criticism."
15. Gleason L. Archer Jr., *A Survey of Old Testament Introduction*, rev. ed. (Chicago: Moody, 1974), 23–25.
16. Roger R. Nicole, "The Nature of Inerrancy," in *Inerrancy and Common Sense*, ed. Roger R. Nicole and J. Ramsey Michaels (Grand Rapids: Baker, 1980), 76.

article that, though perfectly spelled, is written by a dishonest person. While it is important to recognize the possible existence of errors in the ancient manuscripts, early translations, and even modern editions,[17] this in no way destroys the credibility of the inspired Scriptures, whether of the Old or New Testament. The vast majority of the Old Testament text is certain, and the variants that do exist can in most cases be resolved into primary and secondary readings.[18]

Surely anyone who affirms the inspiration and authority of Scripture should be most interested in discovering which one of the several variants in extant texts represents the original wording of Scripture.[19] It is hoped that this book may help many students and pastors chart their way through this difficult but important area of biblical studies.

17. One of the editions of the Authorized (King James) Version was called the "Wicked Bible" because, due to a typesetting error, it rendered the seventh commandment (Exod. 20:14) as "Thou shalt commit adultery."

18. A primary reading is the reading that represents the original. A secondary reading is one that developed from the original through the various imperfections of scribal practice.

19. Roger Beckwith, *The Old Testament Canon of the New Testament Church and Its Background in Early Judaism* (Grand Rapids: Eerdmans/London: SPCK, 1985), 5, makes two interesting statements about the areas of canon and textual criticism. He says that "with no canon there is no Bible" and "with no *text* there is no Bible." The principle of *sola Scriptura* depends on an adequate understanding of canon and a clearly defined text of Scripture.

1

Writing in the Ancient Near East

Study of the transmission of the Old Testament text deals, in large measure, with the origin of Hebrew writing and its development through time. But the field of Hebrew writing is just one small part of a fascinating area of study, the history of writing within human civilization. Clearly, within the scope of this book, no in-depth account of the history of writing can be offered. Yet it will be important to trace at least some of the main features of this story in order to understand more fully the details of the transmission of the Old Testament text. This chapter is given, therefore, to a brief survey of writing in the ancient Near East and to a summary of the place of writing within the confines of the Old Testament itself.

Sumerian Writing

The history of writing in the ancient Near East begins with the Sumerians toward the end of the fourth millennium B.C.[1] This non-Semitic people either invented writing or adopted a writing system from another people. If writing was not totally

1. The date is usually listed as ca. 3100 B.C. The material in this section is based on several standard histories of writing. For more information, the reader should consult one of the following: David Diringer, *The Alphabet*, 3d ed. (London: Hutchison, 1968); idem, *Writing* (London: Thames & Hudson, 1962); Godfrey R. Driver, *Semitic Writing: From Pictograph to Alphabet* (London: Oxford University Press, 1948); Ignace J. Gelb, *A Study of Writing*, 2d ed. (Chicago: University of Chicago Press, 1963).

a Sumerian invention, at least they made major strides in its early development.[2] The Sumerian system of writing, in its earliest stages, was pictographic, that is, signs were used to picture specific objects and thus call them to mind. Pictographic writing, though a start, is limited in what it can represent. At an early stage, therefore, the Sumerians improved their writing by using one sign to refer to several different things. A basic sign that indicated "star" was also used to indicate "sky," "a god," and the adjective "high."[3] The gain that resulted from this development was somewhat offset by ambiguity in what was expressed.

The Sumerians also made another major advance in writing when they began to use some signs to represent syllables. For instance, they used a sign to represent the phonogram ME, an indicator of the plural in Sumerian.[4] Thus, by the time of its classical stage, Sumerian made use of three kinds of signs: pictograms that had as their origin a sign depicting a concrete object, ideograms (called by some word-signs) that could also be used to refer to related objects or concepts, and syllabograms that were used to refer to a specific syllabic sound.[5]

The major shortcoming of the Sumerian system is the large number of signs that were necessary to express thought.[6] A second weakness of the system is the existence of polyphones and homophones.[7] Two additional features of the Sumerian

2. Diringer, *Alphabet*, 20.
3. Driver, *Semitic Writing*, 57.
4. Ibid.
5. Diringer, *Alphabet*, 18.
6. This same drawback is observed in the later Akkadian writing system that was developed from the Sumerian system (see the next subsection). The Akkadian system, in its classical stage, consisted of some 600 to 700 different signs. Contrast the tremendous difficulty of learning to read and write in such a system with the relative ease of the process using an alphabet of 26 letters. Cf. Diringer, *Writing*, 42.
7. A polyphone is a single sign that can have more than one phonetic value. Diringer, *Writing*, 40, gives as an illustration a sign that had ten phonetic values and four ideographic values. An analogy in English is the letter sequence *ough*. The same sequence yields at least seven different sounds: plough, rough, hiccough, hough, cough, through, and though. A homophone is a given phonetic value that is represented by two or more different symbols. Diringer illustrates with GAR, which was represented by fourteen different signs. An analogous situation in English can be observed in the use of *thru* as a variant of *through*.

language were developed to combat this ambiguity. Specialized signs, called determinatives, were placed before or after words to indicate the general class of object or person, etc. For example, there was a determinative for deity, another for certain human occupations, and the like.[8] A second special sign, called a phonetic complement, was also used to enhance clarity in communication. Say that a sign could be read GUL or SUN. The Sumerians would write GUL.UL, where GUL is the ambiguous sign, and UL is the phonetic complement. The phonetic complement was not pronounced, but it ensured that the reader would understand GUL and not SUN.[9] Perhaps an illustration in English would be helpful. Assume for a moment that the letters *sn* represent a single symbol rather than two letters. This symbol, *sn*, could serve to indicate either sun or son. To avoid ambiguity the symbol could be written *snon* for son and *snun* for sun. The system may strike the modern reader as cumbersome, but it provided a workable solution in its time.

Akkadian Writing

The Akkadians, a Semitic people, took over the Sumerian system of writing sometime in the middle of the third millennium B.C. It must be remembered that the Sumerians were not Semitic. Therefore, the Akkadians adopted a script of another, unrelated language and used it to express their own language. The major change introduced by the Akkadians was a much greater use of syllabic signs. Their writing system was not exclusively syllabic, however. Their six hundred to seven hundred signs included the following: six signs to represent vowels, ninety-seven signs that represented "open" syllables (consonant + vowel or vowel + consonant), more than two hundred signs that indicated "closed" syllables (consonant + vowel + consonant), and about three hundred signs that were used as ideograms.[10] The ideograms were essentially the signs

8. Ibid.
9. Gelb, *Study of Writing*, 71.
10. Diringer, *Writing*, 42.

that the Sumerians had used before them, but they were probably pronounced as Akkadian words when the texts were read.
Something analogous occurs when an English speaker reads
$2.00 as "two dollars." A Spanish speaker would read the same
symbols as "dos dólares." Our modern numeral symbols are
simply current examples of ideograms.[11]

The Akkadian language is important for biblical studies on
several levels. In the first place, Akkadian is the earliest attested Semitic language, and its decipherment and study
since the nineteenth century have proved helpful for the elu-
cidation of features of the Hebrew language.[12] The existence
of the Akkadian writing system from the middle of the third
millennium B.C. onward sets the writing activity of various
Old Testament personages in a proper historical and linguistic context. Creation and flood accounts in the Babylonian dialect of Akkadian provide material with which to compare
and contrast the biblical analogs, while Akkadian legal documents, royal annals, and correspondence provide historical
and cultural information.

Egyptian Writing

Though many other ancient Near Eastern writing systems
cannot be included because of limited space, at least one
more needs to be mentioned before speaking briefly of the origin of alphabetic writing. The writing system of ancient
Egypt is known as hieroglyphic writing.[13] This earliest Egyp-

11. Other examples of modern ideograms include a variety of "picture"
signs used along roadways and streets to convey information to travelers,
whatever their mother tongue. An outline of a phone signifies telephone,
teléfono, etc., to travelers.
12. Cf. Sabatino Moscati et al., *An Introduction to the Comparative Grammar of the Semitic Languages* (Wiesbaden: Harrassowitz, 1969), 5. The entire
book is devoted to showing how the grammar of any single Semitic language
can illuminate possibly misunderstood features in another related language.
13. Two later forms, hieratic and demotic, are more cursive in form than
the "picture writing" of the hieroglyphics; cf. Gelb, *Study of Writing*, 75. A still
later form of Egyptian, written with Greek letters, is known as Coptic; cf.
Cyrus H. Gordon, *Forgotten Scripts*, rev. ed. (New York: Basic Books, 1982),
22–23.

tian writing system dates from around 3000 B.C. The system is definitely pictographic and is probably related in some way to Sumerian writing. The signs used in Egypt were not the same as those used in Mesopotamia, so the borrowing is probably not direct. The process may be characterized by the term *stimulus diffusion*.[14]

Certain other features of Egyptian also set it apart from Mesopotamian languages. In the first place, Egyptian hieroglyphic writing maintained its pictographic character throughout its history. Even the cursive forms known as hieratic and demotic, though somewhat more stylized than hieroglyphic, were still basically picture writing. They never developed to the same extent that Akkadian writing did, that is, with a complete loss of similarity to the original pictographs. A second difference between Egyptian and Mesopotamian writing relates to the representation of vowels. Some vowels were written in Mesopotamian scripts, but no vowels were expressed in writing in Egyptian. This feature is shared with early writing habits for Biblical Hebrew and certain other Semitic languages.[15]

Alphabetic Writing

The final stage in the history of writing is the development of a true alphabetic script. Earlier scripts were based on pic-

14. Gordon, *Forgotten Scripts*, 19–20.

15. Diringer, *Writing*, 48–49, says regarding representations of vowels, "The most immediately striking fact about Egyptian writing is that, as in the later Semitic alphabets, only consonants were actually written down: no vowel-sounds were represented. This has nothing to do with the idea which is frequently expressed, that vowels were 'unimportant' in the Hamito-Semitic languages, though they played a more subsidiary role than in the Indo-European tongues. In any oral reading from inscriptions or manuscripts *all* the unwritten vowels would have to be pronounced, and pronounced correctly, for the narrative to be understood. It is simply incorrect to assume that a written script whose particular economy is the non-representation of vowels poses any particular difficulty for those accustomed to reading it, and a smpl tst 'f ths srt shld shw ths qut wll." This understanding of writing or not writing vowels will be important when the work of the Masoretes is discussed in chapter 2.

tograms, ideograms, or syllabograms. The alphabetic script
uses individual letters to represent single sounds of speech.[16]
As such, the alphabet is the most highly developed, the most
convenient, and the most easily adaptable of all systems of
writing ever developed. The use of the alphabet can be acquired by any child with relative ease.[17]

The specific details of the development of the alphabet, at
least in terms of the who, when, and where, are difficult to
pin down. However, at least some answers are generally
agreed on. In terms of the "who," scholars usually have
named the Phoenicians. This indicates that the "where" was
in the general area of Palestine. The Greeks adopted and
adapted the Phoenician script as the basis of their own alphabet in the tenth or ninth century B.C.[18] This implies that
the origin of the Phoenician alphabet must be earlier than
the tenth century. Yet there is additional evidence that allows the date to be located even earlier. Numerous tablets
found at Ugarit are usually dated in the fourteenth century
B.C. They include texts written in Ugaritic, a Semitic language recorded in alphabetic script. The alphabet used in
these texts must have existed before that time, and some
have suggested that this means that a general Semitic alphabet (or proto-alphabet) must have existed in at least the sixteenth or fifteenth century B.C.[19]

Albright, in his work on the Proto-Sinaitic inscriptions,
suggests an alternative to the previously mentioned consensus. Rather than locating the earliest alphabet among the
Phoenicians, he locates it among the Semites who worked in
Egyptian mines in the Sinai Peninsula ca. 1550–1450 B.C. He

16. Gelb, *Study of Writing*, 166.
17. Diringer, *Alphabet*, 13. He adds that the same basic alphabet is used
today by writers of English, French, Italian, German, Spanish, Portuguese,
Turkish, Polish, Dutch, Czech, Croatian, Welsh, Finnish, and Hungarian,
among others.
18. Diringer, *Writing*, 131, 149.
19. Ibid., 116. Driver, *Semitic Writing*, 156, mentions the mixture of Phoenician, Aramaic, and Hebrew names for the letters of the Hebrew alphabet
and suggests that this points to a general development of the Semitic alphabet before the complete separation of the Semitic dialects into different language groups. This evidence supports, in a general way, the suggested dating
for the origin of the alphabet in Palestine.

indicates that "the Proto-Sinaitic inscriptions [can be set] squarely in an evolutionary sequence of letter forms beginning in the 17th century B.C. and extending down into the Iron Age."[20] The principle of this early alphabet is acrophonic, and the Proto-Sinaitic inscriptions attest twenty-three (possibly twenty-five) out of a possible twenty-seven phonemes that were indicated in an early phase of Semitic scripts.[21] If Albright is right, "we may ultimately find ourselves forced back into the Twelfth [Egyptian] Dynasty for the origin of our alphabet."[22]

The changes in the manner of writing from the days of the discovery of the alphabet to the present have been quantitative, not qualitative.[23] The difficulties inherent in earlier systems of writing were largely removed by the invention of the alphabet. Table 1 indicates the ease with which various writing systems were used.[24]

20. William F. Albright, *The Proto-Sinaitic Inscriptions and Their Decipherment*, Harvard Theological Studies 22 (Cambridge: Harvard University Press, 1966), 6, 10.

21. Ibid., 2–3. The acrophonic principle refers to the use of a symbol that represents a word to identify the sound of the first consonant of the word. For example, the early form of the Hebrew letter *bet* pictured a house and was used to indicate the *b* sound. The acrophonic principle is used in some kinds of puzzles where the initial letters of several words spell a new word. The words *boy*, *art*, *newspaper*, and *dog*, via their first letters, spell the word *band*.

22. Ibid., 15. The Twelfth Dynasty dates to ca. 1983–1786; see Kenneth A. Kitchen, "Egypt, History of (Chronology)," in *The Anchor Bible Dictionary*, ed. David N. Freedman et al. (New York: Doubleday, 1992), 2:329.

23. Early writing in the Proto-Sinaitic inscriptions was in single vertical columns read from top to bottom. Other arrangements are also found (Albright, *Proto-Sinaitic Inscriptions*, 8). As is well known, Hebrew is written from right to left rather than from left to right as in English. Some ancient Greek was written in what is called boustrophedon, that is, the lines read from right to left on one line and left to right on the next:

What started from left to
morf deunitnoc saw thgir
right to left, etc.

But these variations in writing are superficial, not substantive.

24. An example of a modern language that is based on ideographic principles is Japanese. There are approximately 2,000 official ideograms, but the total number is more like 5,000. Cf. "Ejecutivos a Japón," *La Vanguardia*, 20 April 1991, 64.

TABLE 1 WRITING SYSTEMS

Language	Total Signs	Syllabic Signs
Sumerian	ca. 600	ca. 100–150
Egyptian	ca. 700	ca. 100
Hittite	450+	ca. 60
Chinese	ca. 50,000	—
Persian	41	—
Ugaritic	30	—
Hebrew	22	—
English	26	—

Sources: Ignace J. Gelb, A Study of Writing, 2d ed. (Chicago: University of Chicago Press, 1963), 115, 129; and David Diringer, Writing (London: Thames & Hudson, 1962), 111.

Writing in the Old Testament

In highlighting the importance of the history of human writing to the issue of writing in the Old Testament and, ultimately, to the matter of the textual transmission of the Old Testament text, it is important to emphasize the great antiquity of writing. As mentioned before, both Sumerian and Egyptian were well-developed writing systems around 3100 to 3000 B.C. This antedates Moses, the earliest of Old Testament writers, by at least fifteen hundred years.[25] But even more can be said. According to the Old Testament, Moses was reared in Pharaoh's court. It is therefore well within reasonable limits to suppose that Moses knew how to read and write, not only his own native Hebrew (Canaanite) language, but also Egyptian hieroglyphics.[26] Also, based on the existence of

25. I hold that the early date of the exodus fits best with all the available biblical and archeological data. On the basis of a late date for the exodus, there is even more time between the first appearance of writing and the time of Moses.

26. Cf. Terence C. Mitchell, The Bible in the British Museum: Interpreting the Evidence (London: British Museum, 1988), 31.

the Tell el-Amarna tablets, Moses may well have been able to read and write Akkadian.[27] This is a far cry from what some scholars used to assert—that Moses could not have written the Pentateuch because he could not read and write!

Second, it is important to place the question of the role of oral transmission in the production of the Old Testament within its ancient Near Eastern context. No doubt oral transmission played some role in ancient Egypt and Mesopotamia, but its importance may well have been overstressed by an earlier generation of scholars. The vast numbers of papyrus documents and clay tablets that have been unearthed in the past several centuries in these centers bear eloquent testimony to the importance of written documents from the very earliest stages of graphic communication.[28]

Finally, the availability of an alphabetic script for the earliest writing of the Old Testament books must not be undervalued. What would have been much more difficult through the means of cuneiform or hieroglyphic writing was, in fact, greatly facilitated by the existence of an alphabetic script. And not only that, but the availability of the Old Testament to its readership would have also been *very* limited had it been written in the systems of Mesopotamia or Egypt.[29]

27. Akkadian was the *lingua franca* throughout the ancient Near East during the so-called Amarna Age. Local officials in Syria and Palestine wrote to the Egyptian rulers in Akkadian during the fifteenth and fourteenth centuries B.C. Cf. Gordon, *Forgotten Scripts*, 82–83; and Driver, *Semitic Writing*, 103. Note the reference to Moses' education in Acts 7:22, "Moses was educated in all the wisdom of the Egyptians and was powerful in speech and action" (New International Version).

28. Diringer, *Writing*, 14, comments as follows: "The possibilities inherent in oral transmission are far wider than was conceived a century or two ago, but in comparison with the worlds opened up by the use of writing, they are bounded by fixed and absolute limits." Kenneth A. Kitchen, *Ancient Orient and Old Testament* (Downers Grove, Ill.: InterVarsity, 1966), 135–36, makes a crucial distinction between oral dissemination of a document to contemporaries and oral transmission of a document through time. For the transmission of important documents to posterity, people of the ancient Near East usually resorted to written communication.

29. Driver, *Semitic Writing*, 3, observes that writing (and presumably reading) in both Egypt and Mesopotamia was the province of a limited number who were part of a priestly class. This state of affairs should be con-

Conclusion

This chapter has surveyed the history of writing from the first systems of pictographic script to the final, and fortuitous, invention of the alphabet (see table 2 for representative samples of early cuneiform and alphabetic signs; see table 3 for a summary of the history of writing). The place of writing in the Old Testament fits very nicely within the overall context of the ancient Near East. The existence of an alphabetic script

TABLE 2   CUNEIFORM AND ALPHABETIC SIGNS

	Sample Sign	Value
Sumerian (pictograph)		SAG ("head")
Sumerian (cuneiform)		SAG ("head")
Akkadian (Classical Neo-Assyrian)		rêšu ("head")
Egyptian (pictogram and determinative)		tp ("head")
Ugaritic		r
Paleo-Hebrew		r

Sources: René Labat and Florence Malbran-Labat, Manuel d'Épigraphie Akkadienne (Signes, Syllabaire, Idéogrammes), 6th ed. (Paris: Geuthner, 1988), 90–91 [Sumerian and Akkadian]; Alan H. Gardiner, Egyptian Grammar, 3d. ed. (Oxford: Griffith Institute, Ashmolean Museum, 1957), 449 [Egyptian]; Cyrus H. Gordon, Ugaritic Textbook, Analecta Orientalia 38 (Rome: Pontifical Biblical Institute Press, 1965), 15 [Ugaritic]; Emil Kautzsch, Gesenius' Hebrew Grammar, trans. Arthur E. Cowley, 2d ed. (Oxford: Clarendon, 1910), "Table of Early Alphabets," following page xvi [paleo-Hebrew].

trasted with the testimony of the Old Testament. According to Deut. 17:18–19, an Israelite king was to make and read from a personal copy of the Torah. Additionally, in Judg. 8:14, a young man (a young lad?) wrote out a list of over seventy names of the princes and elders of Succoth. These kinds of activities would not have been normal for Egyptian and Mesopotamian life.

TABLE 3 HISTORY OF WRITING

Language	Major Features
Sumerian (from ca. 3100 B.C.)	pictograms ideograms syllabograms determinatives phonetic complements
Egyptian (from ca. 3000 B.C.)	pictographic vowels not represented in writing
Akkadian (from ca. 2500 B.C.)	ideograms signs for vowels signs for syllables earliest attested Semitic language
Proto-Sinaitic (ca. 1550–1450 B.C.)	early stage of alphabet development
Ugaritic (ca. 14th century B.C.)	alphabetic cuneiform script
Phoenician (from ca. 12th century B.C.)	further development of alphabet

greatly facilitated the recording of divine revelation in written form. We turn next to a description of the history of the transmission of the Old Testament text in the Hebrew language.

2

Transmission of the Old Testament in Hebrew

Any attempt to trace the important features in the transmission of the Old Testament text in the Hebrew language[1] must deal with a vast time period. According to the traditional view, the Old Testament Scriptures were produced from the time of Moses to the time of Malachi, that is, from about 1400 B.C. to around 400 B.C.[2] This indicates that even during the Old Testament epoch the text of each Old Testament book had to be repeatedly copied by hand to ensure its preservation for posterity. This hand copying, as the sole means of textual transmission, continued from the end of the Old Testament epoch until the invention of the printing press in the fifteenth century A.D. The earliest printed text of the entire Old Testament was produced in Soncino, Italy, in A.D. 1488.[3] This means that the oldest parts of the Old Testament were transmitted by hand copying for nearly three thousand years before they

1. The Samaritan Pentateuch, though written in Hebrew, is discussed in chapter 3 for reasons that are mentioned there.
2. Modern scholarship typically dates the earliest of the so-called Pentateuchal sources to the tenth century B.C. and the latest of the Old Testament books to Maccabean times. From a strictly *text-critical* view, the different dating systems are not very significant. With either date, the Old Testament documents were copied by hand through the entire period up to the fifteenth century A.D. For a defense of the traditional date of Old Testament books see Gleason L. Archer Jr., *A Survey of Old Testament Introduction*, 2d ed. (Chicago: Moody, 1974); or Roland K. Harrison, *Old Testament Introduction* (Grand Rapids: Eerdmans, 1969).
3. Ernst Würthwein, *The Text of the Old Testament*, trans. Erroll F. Rhodes (Grand Rapids: Eerdmans, 1979), 37.

were first put in printed form. Even the most recent Old Testament books were transmitted manually for about two thousand years before they were printed. Since the Old Testament text was copied by hand over such a vast amount of time, it is important to know as much as possible about this process.

History of the Transmission of the Old Testament in Hebrew

Among the various ways that the history of the transmission of the Old Testament text in Hebrew could be schematized, the discussion to follow is organized according to five historical eras.

Textual Transmission Prior to 300 B.C.

Very little direct evidence exists concerning textual transmission in the earliest time period.[4] Since this period covers an important phase of the transmission of the Old Testament text, however, some features of its inferred history should be mentioned. A variety of evidence indicates that the Old Testament books were first written and copied in the Phoenician (or paleo-Hebrew) script.[5] The square (or Aramaic) script replaced this archaic script toward the end of the period. Since different sets of letters could be easily confused in the two scripts, *both* must be considered as a potential source of copying error in Old Testament texts (see table 4).[6] As a final comment, Jesus' reference in Matthew 5:18 to the *yôd* as the smallest letter of the Law clearly indicates that the square, or Aramaic, script was in common use in Palestine in the first century A.D.

4. Shemaryahu Talmon, "The Old Testament Text," in *The Cambridge History of the Bible*, vol. 1: *From the Beginnings to Jerome*, ed. Peter R. Ackroyd and Christopher F. Evans (Cambridge: Cambridge University Press, 1970), 159.
    5. Würthwein, *Text of the Old Testament*, 4.
    6. Aage Bentzen, *Introduction to the Old Testament* (Copenhagen: Gad, 1948), 1:46; Bleddyn J. Roberts, *The Old Testament Text and Versions* (Cardiff: University of Wales Press, 1951), 92–93. See also the further discussion in chapter 6 of this book.

TABLE 4   EXAMPLES OF LETTERS CONFUSED IN THE OLD AND SQUARE SCRIPTS

Paleo-Hebrew	*bêt*	*dālet*
	ᕱ	◁
	kap	*mēm*
	𐤉	𐤌
Square Script	*bêt*	*kap*
	ב	כ
	dālet	*rêš*
	ד	ר

Source: Emil Kautzsch, *Genesius' Hebrew Grammar*, trans. Arthur E. Cowley, 2d ed. (Oxford: Clarendon, 1910), "Table of Early Alphabets," following page xvi.

Another feature of this early phase involves the transmission of texts as individual scrolls and not as parts of a codex (or book form).[7] Scrolls were made of either leather or papyrus. The standard size of papyrus scrolls was on the order of ten inches high by about thirty feet long, which was enough to accommodate the text of Isaiah. This standard scroll size was likely the reason for the division of the Pentateuch into five parts of more or less equal size.[8] The Old Testament books of Samuel, Kings, and Chronicles, all considered single books by the Jews, were each able to be written in Hebrew on a single scroll. In the Septuagint, each of these books had to

7. The codex was introduced in the second century A.D. for private copies of the Old Testament, but the scroll form continued to be used in synagogues. Cf. Ernst Sellin, *Introduction to the Old Testament*, rev. Georg Fohrer, trans. David E. Green (Nashville: Abingdon, 1968), 492.

8. The Pentateuch would have been copied on five scrolls because it did not fit on a single scroll. This feature should not obscure its unified composition. In modern terminology we would refer to it as a work published in five volumes.

be written on two scrolls because Greek writing (with consonants *and vowels*) takes more space than Hebrew. This feature required the division of these three books into the now
well-known sets of two books each.[9]
     Text transmission prior to 300 B.C. was also based on a pre-
dominantly consonantal spelling. As initially written, most
early Old Testament books would have been written in an exclusively consonantal text. From about the ninth century on,
certain consonants came to be used to indicate vowels. These
"helping" consonants are called *matres lectionis*, literally
"mothers of reading." They were first used to indicate final
long vowels (beginning in the ninth century B.C.), and later (beginning in the eighth century B.C.) they were also used to indicate medial long vowels. *Matres lectionis* were subsequently
added to the Old Testament text, but not in a completely systematic way. The process of adding vowel letters continued
through time, but the later proto-Masoretic Text reflected an
earlier, less developed, stage in the use of vowel letters than
what is reflected in the Qumran scrolls (the majority of Qumran biblical scrolls date from the last two centuries B.C.).[10]
     The traditional view of the transmission of the Hebrew text
before 300 B.C. included a fourth feature: the supposed practice of continuous writing (i.e., writing without spaces or dividing marks between words). This practice, if indeed it was
standard, would obviously have increased the chances for errors in the transmission and subsequent translation of the
text.[11] Some authors suggest that the Septuagint translators

     9. See also the discussion of the Septuagint and related versions in chap-
ter 3 of this book.
     10. Cf. David N. Freedman, "The Massoretic Text and the Qumran
Scrolls: A Study in Orthography," in *Qumran and the History of the Biblical
Text*, ed. Frank M. Cross and Shemaryahu Talmon (Cambridge: Harvard University Press, 1975), 196–211.
     11. See, e.g., Roberts, *Old Testament Text*, 93, who states that "another
source of textual corruption was the absence of word-division in the text in
both the Canaanite and the Aramaic script, with a resultant possible diver-
gent division of words and the consequent adoption of erroneous readings."
Cf. also Christian D. Ginsburg, *Introduction to the Massoretico-Critical Edition of the Hebrew Bible* (London: Trinitarian Bible Society, 1897; reprinted
with prolegomenon by Harry M. Orlinsky: New York: Ktav, 1966), 158–59, for
a similar approach.

(ca. 250 to 150 B.C.) used Hebrew texts written in continuous script. However, the biblical scrolls found at Qumran, both those written in paleo-Hebrew and those written in the square script, clearly show that words were separated.[12] The picture that we now have of ancient Semitic writing is that word division was the rule, and continuous writing was the exception.[13] This revised understanding of the ancient writing practices of Hebrew scribes is confirmed by the scribal procedures in Ugaritic texts, where word division was usually indicated by a small vertical wedge-shaped stroke.[14] The cases of misdivision of words that have been cited in previous treatments of Old Testament textual criticism are not to be denied. Rather they are to be seen as perhaps the result of occasional crowding in the scribe's *Vorlage* that would have obliterated the marking of word division. Had the entire Old Testament text existed in *scriptio continua* there would likely have been many more cases of misdivision than is actually the case.[15]

A final feature of the transmission of the Hebrew text before 300 B.C has to do with a major revision of Hebrew grammar around 1350 B.C.[16] This means that the earliest books of the Old Testament must have been revised subsequent to this date since the grammar of the Old Testament is more or less standard throughout.[17]

12. Alan R. Millard, " 'Scriptio Continua' in Early Hebrew: Ancient Practice or Modern Surmise?" *Journal of Semitic Studies* 15 (1970): 10, who indicates that, in paleo-Hebrew texts, word division was indicated by points; in square script by spaces.

13. Ibid., 12–13.

14. Cyrus H. Gordon, *Ugaritic Textbook* (Rome: Pontifical Biblical Institute Press, 1965), 15, 23. The word divider was sometimes omitted at the end of a line of text.

15. Emanuel Tov, *Textual Criticism of the Hebrew Bible* (Minneapolis: Fortress, 1992), 8, 208–9, 252, basically agrees with this position, but leaves open the question of the existence of continuously written originals.

16. Bruce K. Waltke, "The Textual Criticism of the Old Testament," in *Expositor's Bible Commentary*, ed. Frank E. Gaebelein (Grand Rapids: Zondervan, 1979); 1:213. An updated version of Waltke's article may be found in Bruce K. Waltke and Michael O'Connor, *An Introduction to Biblical Hebrew Syntax* (Winona Lake, Ind.: Eisenbrauns, 1990), 15–28.

17. It is true that some grammatical differences are reflected in the Old Testament corpus. Cyrus H. Gordon (unpublished class notes on the Hebrew

In summary, the Old Testament text was updated in several ways during the period from the writing of individual books until 300 B.C. Books initially written and copied in an archaic script were later copied and transmitted in the square script. Old Testament books were copied individually on scrolls throughout this era. The spelling of the Old Testament text was also upgraded throughout this stage by the introduction of vowel letters (*matres lectionis*). Occasional crowding of a portion of text, whichever script was used, would have sometimes led to incorrect word division as the text was copied during this period. Also, at least in the case of the earliest books, the grammar was revised to reflect conventions that were current subsequent to 1350 B.C. Most scholars agree, however, that this grammatical revision did not change the content of the Old Testament. This conclusion is based on the self-understanding of the Israelite people regarding Scripture (see Deut. 4:2 and 13:1 [Engl. 12:32]) and the analogy with ancient Near Eastern scribal practices.[18]

Textual Transmission from 300 B.C. to A.D. 135

The history of the Old Testament text during the period 300 B.C. to A.D. 135 is pivotal to the entire history of the Hebrew Scriptures.[19] One of the primary reasons for this importance is that there is now clear manuscript evidence for this time period. What was only inferential for the preceding phase of the history of the transmission of the text is now direct.

Pride of place for the manuscript evidence of this phase belongs to the Qumran biblical manuscripts. It is true that many of the manuscripts are fragmentary, but even so, their impor-

---

language, New York University, fall 1987) mentions four classes of differences: temporal, local (i.e., dialect), genre, and individual (i.e., author). These differences are relatively minor and more in the nature of variations from the common core of Old Testament grammar.

18. Waltke, "Textual Criticism," 212.

19. Talmon, "Old Testament Text," 165. Moshe H. Goshen-Gottstein, "Hebrew Biblical Manuscripts," in *Qumran and the History of the Biblical Text*, ed. Frank M. Cross and Shemaryahu Talmon (Cambridge: Harvard University Press, 1975), 48, calls this period "four decisive centuries" in the history of the Old Testament text.

tance is noteworthy because these manuscripts have been dated to the period between the third and the first centuries B.C., with the majority belonging to the second and first centuries.[20] Prior to the discovery of these manuscripts, beginning in 1947, the only access to the practices of this period was through inferences drawn from the study of the early versions. The Qumran scrolls give direct access to scribal activity in these crucial centuries. All of the Old Testament books are represented among the Qumran documents with the exception of Esther.[21]

The Qumran scrolls are discussed in detail in chapter 4. Here I only highlight results of the study of the Qumran biblical manuscripts in Hebrew. The primary feature of these Old Testament manuscripts is that they give evidence of a multiplicity of text families or groups. Some manuscripts are closely parallel to what later became known as the Masoretic Text. Other Qumran manuscripts are similar to the textual tradition of the Septuagint, and still others resemble the textual tradition of the Samaritan Pentateuch.[22] Thus the main result of the Qumran finds is the certification of what before had been only an inference from the study of the versions. The Hebrew text of the Old Testament existed, in the period under consideration, in a variety of textual traditions or text families.

Other Hebrew manuscripts from this same time frame were found near the Wadi Murabbaʿat, south of Qumran. These finds date from the time of the rebellion of Bar-Kochba (about A.D. 135). Their main distinguishing feature is general agreement with the text form later known as Masoretic.[23] Thus the multiplicity of text types evident at Qumran between

20. Talmon, "Old Testament Text," 183.
21. Frank M. Cross, *The Ancient Library of Qumran and Modern Biblical Studies* (Grand Rapids: Baker, 1980), 40.
22. Ibid., 181–86. See also Frank M. Cross, "The Contribution of the Qumran Discoveries to the Study of the Biblical Text," in *Qumran and the History of the Biblical Text*, ed. Frank M. Cross and Shemaryahu Talmon (Cambridge: Harvard University Press, 1975), 279–80, and the discussion in chapter 3 of this book.
23. Talmon, "Old Testament Text," 183.

the third to first centuries B.C. was replaced by a single and authoritative text type by A.D. 135 at the latest. When was this single, authoritative text form of the Old Testament first established? Actually, the question needs to be stated in a more specific form. It is not merely a question of when it was established, but when it was established *in Palestine*. The text that came to be recognized as standard obviously existed long before it was accepted in an official way in Palestine. This standard text was clearly accepted in Palestine sometime before A.D. 135, but it would be desirable to determine a more specific date if possible. It appears that a date early in the first century A.D. is a good candidate, since the standard Hebrew text served as the basis for the *kaige* recension of the Septuagint in Palestine in that time period.[24] There are also those who hold that the standard text was adopted by Jewish scribes in Palestine at an even earlier date. Robert Gordis holds that it was adopted as early as the time of Salome Alexandra (76 to 67 B.C.).[25] Whichever date is accepted for its official recognition in Palestine, it must be remembered that the standard text predates its acceptance. The standard text was *not* a new creation. Rather one text form was selected in preference to two other text forms that also existed at that time.

It will be helpful in summing up this section to briefly highlight the conclusions of Frank M. Cross concerning the Qumran findings (see figure 1). He holds that the data are best explained by a hypothesis of local text types or families.[26] Three

24. A recension is a revision of an ancient text. Cross ("Contribution of the Qumran Discoveries," 291) calls the *kaige* recension the Proto-Theodotionic recension. The *kaige* recension has also been identified by Dominique Barthélemy in the Greek Scroll of the Minor Prophets that was found at Naḥal Ḥever, which Barthélemy refers to as R; see Barthélemy, "Redécouverte d'un Châinon Manquant de l'Histoire de la Septante," in *Qumran and the History of the Biblical Text*, ed. Frank M. Cross and Shemaryahu Talmon (Cambridge: Harvard University Press, 1975), 132. For further discussion, see chapter 3.

25. Robert Gordis, *The Biblical Text in the Making: A Study of the Kethib-Qere*, augmented ed. (New York: Ktav, 1971), xli.

26. Cross's reconstruction of the history of the Old Testament text is not shared by either Shemaryahu Talmon or Emanuel Tov. Talmon stresses the probable existence of many more text types than three. He would explain the

FIGURE 1   THEORY OF LOCAL TEXTS

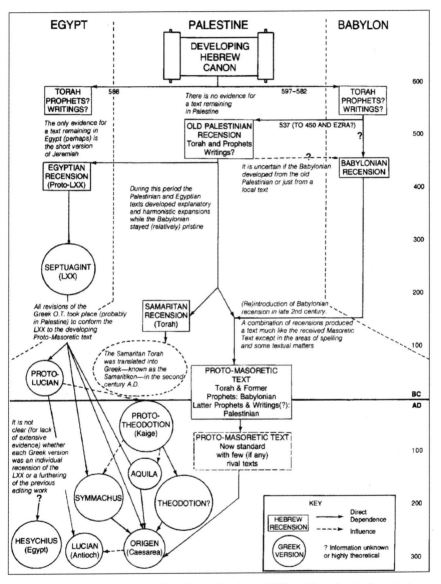

Source: The NIV Triglot Old Testament (Grand Rapids: Zondervan, 1981), xvii. Reproduced with permission.

families of manuscripts are known for the Pentateuch and the Former Prophets, while only two are attested for the Latter Prophets.[27] Cross sketches the probable development of these manuscript families in the following way. Sometime in the fifth century B.C. two local texts began to develop independently in Palestine and Babylon. In the early fourth century B.C. the Egyptian family broke off from the Old Palestinian text and began its own independent development. The Egyptian text served as the *Vorlage* for the translation of the Septuagint in the third to second centuries B.C. The Palestinian family was reflected in the Samaritan Pentateuch. The Babylonian manuscript type may have come back into Palestine as early as Maccabean times. By the first century B.C. or the early first century A.D. it became accepted as the official form of the Pentateuch and the Former Prophets within Jewish scribal circles. It was apparently not available in the case of the Latter Prophets, so the Palestinian text type was adopted for these books. This accepted standard text replaced the other families, except as they were reflected in the Septuagint and the Samaritan Pentateuch, and would later be called the Masoretic Text.[28]

---

three known to current scholarship as those that survived from the larger number that must have existed at a yet earlier stage; see Talmon, "The Textual Study of the Bible—A New Outlook," in *Qumran and the History of the Biblical Text*, ed. Frank M. Cross and Shemaryahu Talmon (Cambridge: Harvard University Press, 1975), 324–25. Tov agrees with Talmon in part, but he emphasizes that the three currently known text forms should be seen as three surviving *texts* (emphasis his) and not as recensions or text types; see Tov, "A Modern Textual Outlook Based on the Qumran Scrolls," *Hebrew Union College Annual* 53 (1982): 11. As an approximation, Cross's outlook is more Lagardian, while Talmon's and Tov's can be described as more Kahlian. (These terms derive from the views of Paul de Lagarde and Paul Kahle: Lagarde held that there was a single archetype from which all Old Testament manuscripts derived; Kahle espoused a theory of "vulgar" texts, i.e., a plurality of text forms.) Part of the problem may be that some scholars focus on the similarities between manuscripts (Cross), while others focus on their differences (Talmon and Tov). My view is that Cross is basically correct in his understanding of text history. It may be necessary, however, to revise certain details of his theory in the light of the criticisms of Talmon and Tov.

27. Cross, "Contribution of the Qumran Discoveries," 281.
28. Ibid., 290–92. See also the following section of this chapter.

Textual Transmission from A.D. 135 to 1000

In the period ending in A.D. 135 there was a move from a plurality of text types to the adoption of a standard text within Jewish scribal circles. In the next phase the primary focus is on the transmission of that standard text. The period can be conveniently broken into two parts: the transmission of the standard text by Jewish rabbis from A.D. 135 to 500 and the textual activities of the Masoretes from A.D. 500 to 1000.

A.D. 135 to 500. The time period A.D. 135–500 corresponds roughly to what may be called the age of the Talmud. It is probable that the division of the text into verses, a feature taken for granted by the modern reader, occurred during this time.[29] There were variations between Palestinian and Babylonian schools in regard to the total number of verses in individual books and groups of books (i.e., the Pentateuch).[30] By contrast, the division of the Old Testament into chapters, another feature so necessary for modern readers, was not of Jewish origin. Chapter divisions and numbering were of Christian origin and were introduced into Hebrew manuscripts in the time of Rabbi Salomon ben Ishmael (ca. A.D. 1330).[31]

The division of the text into paragraphs probably also dates from the talmudic period. All of the Old Testament books except Psalms were divided into two kinds of paragraphs: open and closed. An open paragraph started on a new line after a complete or partial blank line, while a closed paragraph started on the same line after a small space at the end of the preceding paragraph.[32] In current Old Testament texts these divisions are indicated by the letter ס for open paragraphs and

29. Würthwein, *Text of the Old Testament*, 21; cf. also Bentzen, *Introduction to the Old Testament*, 1:49. Verse division does not necessarily mean verse *numbering*. According to Ginsburg (*Massoretico-Critical Edition*, 107), verse numbers were first included in the Hebrew Bible published at Antwerp in A.D. 1571.

30. Ginsburg, *Massoretico-Critical Edition*, 69; Würthwein, *Text of the Old Testament*, 21.

31. Ginsburg, *Massoretico-Critical Edition*, 25. According to Würthwein (*Text of the Old Testament*, 21), Old Testament chapter divisions were the work of Stephen Langton (1150–1228).

32. Würthwein, *Text of the Old Testament*, 21; Bentzen, *Introduction to the Old Testament*, 1:48–49.

by the letter ס for closed paragraphs (smaller than the surrounding consonantal text).
   Liturgical divisions of the text were also likely made at the
same time. Here again there was a divergence between the
custom in Palestine and that in Babylon. The practice in Palestine was to read through the Torah every three years. For this
purpose the Torah was divided into 452 *Sedarim*. In Babylon
the custom was to read through the Torah every year. Therefore the Babylonian form of the text was divided into 54
Parashoth.[33] Similar divisions were also added to the rest of the
Old Testament.[34] The Palestinian *Sedarim* are indicated in current printed texts by a large letter ס printed in the margin. The
Babylonian *Parashoth* are indicated by פרש in the margin.[35]
   In addition to the verse and textual divisions there are
other textual features that may be dated to the talmudic period.[36] These features include fifteen occasions where a
heavy dot was placed over a letter or word that was in some
way doubtful (e.g., the dot over the *yôd* of the last word in
Gen. 16:5 or the two dots over the accusative particle in
Gen. 37:12).[37] They also include a special vertical stroke
called *paseq* ("divider") that is used some 480 times in the
Old Testament. The specific meaning of this symbol is not
now known.[38] A suspended *nun* is found in Judges 18:30.
Another of these special symbols is an inverted *nun*, which
occurs in Numbers 10:34–36 and Psalm 107:21–26, 40.[39]

   33. Würthwein, *Text of the Old Testament*, 21.
   34. Bentzen, *Introduction to the Old Testament*, 1:49.
   35. For further details, see the discussion in chapter 5.
   36. Cf. the discussion by Israel Yeivin, *Introduction to the Tiberian Masorah*, trans. and ed. E. John Revell (Missoula, Mont.: Scholars Press, 1980),
132, who locates these features in the talmudic era. By way of contrast,
Waltke, "Textual Criticism," 214, locates most of these same features in the
preceding period. Perhaps the textual activity described here was begun in
the earlier period and came to be formalized and finalized in the talmudic
period.
   37. Ginsburg, *Massoretico-Critical Edition*, 318–34. There are ten occasions in the Pentateuch, four in the Prophets, and one in the Writings.
   38. The feature is discussed by Michael Fishbane, *Biblical Interpretation
in Ancient Israel* (Oxford: Clarendon, 1985), 40. He refers to it as *pĕsîq*.
   39. Würthwein, *Text of the Old Testament*, 17; Ginsburg, *Massoretico-Critical Edition*, 334–45.

In addition, blank spaces were left in the middle of twenty-eight verses of the Old Testament text. These blank spaces may signify that some Hebrew text has been omitted in these places.

Finally, there is evidence that certain changes were introduced into the text in order to avoid indelicate expressions and the names of pagan deities. In the cases of indelicate expressions, the consonantal text was not changed. The vowel tradition was changed in order to substitute more acceptable phrasing in the place of the objectionable words.[40] An alternate word was used for personal names that contained the name of a pagan god. Note for example the name Ishbaal (1 Chron. 8:33; 9:39) and its alternate form Ishbosheth (2 Sam. 2:8; 3:8, 15). Ishbaal means "man of Baal," whereas Ishbosheth means "man of shame."[41]

In summary, the main changes during this period were "external" textual features that aided reading and understanding and helped in liturgical use. In some cases, indelicate expressions were avoided through a use of more acceptable synonyms or the substitution of a different word for the name of a pagan deity.

A.D. 500 to 1000. It is in the textual phase following A.D. 500 that we deal with Masoretic activity.[42] This activity was carried out in various places during the time period because of certain historical factors that affected the Jewish people. The triumph of Christianity in Palestine was one of several interrelated factors that caused a large-scale emigration of Jewish textual scholars to Babylon in the second century A.D. The study of the biblical text thrived in several academies in Babylon from the third to the tenth centuries. Two different systems of vocalization were worked out in Babylon, a simple (earlier) system and a complicated (later) system. But neither

---

40. Ginsburg, *Massoretico-Critical Edition*, 345–47; the consonantal text of 2 Kings 18:27 = Isaiah 36:12 speaks of "human excrement" and "urine," but the alternate forms speak of "filth" and "water of their feet."
41. Ibid., 402.
42. "Masoretic" and "Massoretic" alternate in the scholarly literature. "Masoretic" is used in this work.

was destined to be accepted and maintained by later mainstream Jewish textual scholars.[43]

The Islamic conquest of Palestine in A.D. 638 made possible
a revival of Jewish textual work in Tiberias, a city on the
western shore of the Sea of Galilee.[44] It was the work of the
Tiberian Masoretes that would be reflected in the subsequent
study and transmission of the Old Testament text. There was
a simple Palestinian system of vocalization that predated the
Tiberian system, but both the Palestinian and Babylonian systems were superseded by the Tiberian system. As a result,
they were lost to modern scholarship until rediscovered in
the last two centuries, principally through Paul Kahle's work
on the Cairo Geniza materials.[45] Variations between the Tiberian and Babylonian textual traditions are referred to in *BHS*
by the abbreviations Occ (i.e., Western Masoretes, or the
Tiberian tradition) and Or (i.e., Eastern Masoretes, or the
Babylonian tradition).[46]

The contribution of the Tiberian Masoretes needs to be described in some detail. They transmitted the consonantal text
that they had inherited from the talmudic rabbis, but their
most important work was the creation of an overall system to
ensure the accurate understanding of the Old Testament text
and its correct transmission to subsequent generations. This
system consisted of three elements.[47] First was a set of symbols that graphically represented the vowel tradition that had
previously been transmitted only orally. Since the earliest
manuscripts were written in a purely consonantal text, the
reader had to supply the implied vowels in order to read and
understand the texts. Later use of *matres lectionis* was of

---

43. Paul E. Kahle, *The Cairo Geniza*, 2d ed. (Oxford: Blackwell, 1959), 57–
64. See also Solomon Grayzel, *A History of the Jews*, rev. ed. (Philadelphia:
Jewish Publication Society, 1968), 198–200, 206–7, for a discussion of the
other factors involved in this change of the center of gravity of Jewish textual
scholarship.

44. Grayzel, *History of the Jews*, 248–49. Cf. also Max L. Margolis and Alexander Marx, *A History of the Jewish People* (Philadelphia: Jewish Publication Society, 1934), 266.

45. Kahle, *Cairo Geniza*, 57–75.

46. See table 9 (p. 104) and the discussion in chapter 7.

47. Yeivin, *Tiberian Masorah*, 1.

some help in reading and understanding the text, but they were an imperfect system. Therefore the Tiberian Masoretes developed a written system to record more completely the vowel tradition that had been handed down orally through the centuries. What must be stressed at this point is that the Tiberian Masoretes were *conserving* the tradition that they had received with regard to the vowels of the text. They were *not* innovators. Bruce Waltke, following the work of James Barr, summarizes the evidence for this assertion. The Masoretic system of representing the vowel tradition is supported by both Aquila's revision of the Septuagint and Jerome's work in what came to be known as the Latin Vulgate.[48] The Masoretic vowel system is further supported by the clear indication in the Talmud that Jewish scribes learned both a consonantal *and* a vocalic tradition from their teachers. The work of the Masoretes is also supported by the smooth fit of modern Masoretic Text–based grammars within the framework of comparative Semitic grammar. And finally, the Masoretic tradition is supported by the preservation of certain anomalous forms and dialectical differences within the text preserved by the Masoretes.[49]

Second, the Masoretes developed a system of written symbols to record the accentual character of the Hebrew text. These accent marks serve two purposes in Hebrew: they usually mark the accented (stressed) syllable in the words of the text,[50] and they also assist in the reading and understanding of the text. In regard to this latter function, the accents are divided into two systems. One serves for the "twenty-one"

48. For further details, see the discussion in chapter 3.

49. Waltke, "Textual Criticism," 217–18; Waltke and O'Connor, *Biblical Hebrew Syntax*, 26–28. Cf. also the following statement of Moshe H. Goshen-Gottstein, "The Rise of the Tiberian Bible Text," in *The Canon and Masorah of the Hebrew Bible*, ed. Sid Z. Leiman (New York: Ktav, 1974), 681: "In my opinion, the work of the Masoretes, which reached a peak in the Aleppo Codex, is to be understood as the invention and perfection of an ever more refined graphic notation for an age-old oral tradition which endeavored to note down with the greatest possible exactness the smallest details of the customary liturgical way of reading the Bible."

50. Some accents are postpositive (i.e., placed after the stressed syllable) and others are prepositive (placed before the stressed syllable). But the majority of accent marks clearly indicate stress. Cf. further chapter 5.

books (all but the three poetic books), and the other serves for the three poetic books: Psalms, Job, and Proverbs. In addition, the accents are divided into two classes: disjunctive and conjunctive. The major disjunctive accents usually serve to divide the verse into two or more units of thought and are somewhat analogous to commas, semicolons, and periods in English. The conjunctive accents serve to highlight the close attachment of a word to the following word (i.e., that two or more words are to be read without a major pause between them).

Third, the Masoretes developed a system of specialized notes to accompany the text of the Old Testament. They are traditionally grouped into three sections. The Masorah *parva* ("small Masorah") refers to notes written in the side margins of the text. These notes refer to certain word-use statistics for the Old Testament, and they also contain the indications of Kethiv-Qere readings. The Masorah *magna* ("large Masorah") was traditionally recorded in the top and bottom margins of the text. These notes contain a more extensive version of the information contained in the Masorah *parva*. The Masorah *magna* is not printed in *BHS*, but there is a small register between the text proper and the register of textual variants that makes it possible to find the information that is published in a separate series of volumes. The Masorah *magna* register is accessed by small footnote numbers in the Masorah *parva*. These entries then allow access to the separate volumes.[51] There is also a Masorah *finalis* ("final Masorah"), found at the end of biblical books or at the end of sections of the Old Testament (i.e., at the end of the Torah). The Masorah *finalis* contains specialized information about the number of words in the book (or section), the middle word of the book, the middle consonant, etc.[52]

The main contribution of the Masoretes to the development of the Old Testament text thus was the creation of the graphic system to represent vowels, the accent system, and the collection of Masoretic notes. These features were all

51. *BHS*, xiii–xviii. For further details, see chapter 5.
52. William R. Scott, *A Simplified Guide to BHS* (Berkeley: BIBAL, 1987), 9–10.

transmitted along with the text itself. In addition, the Masoretes wrote certain separate works that also had as their goal the correct transmission of the Old Testament text. Among these, the largest is *Ochlah we-Ochlah*, a compilation of some four hundred lists of Masoretic information.[53] The initial list, which gives pairs of words that differ only in the presence or absence of the conjunction *wāw*, is entitled *Ochlah we-Ochlah*, a title that also serves as the title of the complete work. The other lists in this work give information about words and verses that are either identical or differ only in some particular detail.[54] The Cairo Geniza contained other independent Masoretic lists—sometimes general compilations of Masoretic lists or at other times focusing on just a single aspect such as Kethiv-Qere.[55]

Ben Asher and Ben Naphtali. Before surveying some of the most important kinds of information contained in the Masoretic notes, it will be important to mention briefly Aaron ben Asher and Moses ben Naphtali, the last of the Masoretes.[56] These two individuals represented two families of Tiberian Masoretes whose work differed slightly. Since it is the ben Asher text that is the nearest antecedent to the current printed editions of the Old Testament text, it is important to indicate the nature of the differences between these two families.[57] These differences were catalogued by a certain Mishael ben Uzziel in an Arabic work titled *Kitab al-Khilaf.* The Hebrew version of the work is called *Sefer ha-Hillufim.*[58] The differences between ben Asher and ben Naphtali primarily concern details of the accent system. In addition, these two families vary in a few places with regard to spelling, word division, vocalization, use of *dagesh* and *raphe*, vowel quality (i.e., length), and composite versus simple *shewa*.[59] As can be easily seen, these are primarily differences of detail and not of substance.

53. Yeivin, *Tiberian Masorah*, 128.
54. Ibid.
55. Ibid., 127–28.
56. Ibid., 141.
57. Ibid., 18–19.
58. Ibid., 141.
59. Ibid., 142–43.

Kinds of Masoretic Notation. Obviously, a detailed treatment of the information contained in the Masorah is beyond the scope of this work, but it is possible to describe briefly certain key parts of this information. The most important aspect relates to the Kethiv-Qere system. Robert Gordis has cataloged the various kinds of Kethiv-Qere listings.[60] The earliest stage in the development of the Kethiv-Qere readings was the *Qere perpetuum* that substituted Adonai for Yahweh. According to Gordis, this change is found slightly more than 6,800 times in the text, and it was effected before the translation of the Septuagint.[61] A second category of Kethiv-Qere, sixteen in number, aimed at maintaining "clean speech." These were also very early according to Gordis.[62] A third class of Kethiv-Qere readings relates to orthography (i.e., spelling). Of these 259 cases, Gordis indicates that the *plene* form (the form with the vowel letter, or *mater lectionis*) nearly always occurs as the Qere. This type of Kethiv-Qere developed long before the creation of written vowels.[63] Since the Kethiv nearly always preserves the older (archaic) grammatical forms, it is evident that the goal of the Masoretes was not correction or improvement, but rather preservation without change of the text in the form that they had received it.[64] A final category of Kethiv-Qere readings relates to variant readings, numbering in excess of one thousand. Gordis thinks that they are the latest of the Kethiv-Qere readings, and that they were probably developed, by analogy with the preceding cases, when the Masoretes were confronted with variant readings in equally trustworthy manuscripts.[65]

Another type of Masoretic information is called *tiqqune sopherim* ("emendations of the scribes").[66] These eighteen cases, according to the majority Masoretic tradition,[67] appar-

---

60. Gordis, *Biblical Text in the Making*, xvii–xxix.
61. Ibid., xvii. Gordis does not mention it, but the spelling of Jerusalem in the Masoretic Text is also a *Qere perpetuum*.
62. Ibid.
63. Ibid., xix.
64. Ibid., xxviii.
65. Ibid., xxix.
66. Würthwein, *Text of the Old Testament*, 18.
67. There is some variation in ancient Jewish texts with regard to the number of the *tiqqune sopherim*. See Carmel McCarthy, *The Tiqqune Sopher-*

ently arose because of a scribal hesitancy to let certain scriptural statements about God stand unchanged. For instance, according to Masoretic tradition, Genesis 18:22 originally spoke of Yahweh "standing before" Abraham. Since to stand before someone can indicate a sense of subservience, the scribes changed the text to read "Abraham stood before Yahweh."[68]

Finally, another kind of Masoretic notation should be mentioned for completeness: *itture sopherim* ("scribal omissions"). Würthwein seems to use this term to refer to a class of Kethiv-Qere readings.[69] Both Ginsburg and Yeivin, however, distinguish between the *itture sopherim* as a particular category and the classes of Kethiv-Qere.[70] Examples of *itture sopherim* are not encountered in the Book of Ruth, but both of the special types of Kethiv-Qere readings will be illustrated in the textual study of Ruth found in chapter 8.

Textual Transmission from A.D. 1000 to 1450

In the preceding time period the transmission of the Old Testament text was connected with the story of the talmudic rabbis and the Masoretes. Following A.D. 1000, in the period after the Masoretes, the text was transmitted as it was fixed by the Masoretes in terms of its vocalization, accentuation,

---

im and Other Theological Corrections in the Masoretic Text of the Old Testament, Orbis Biblicus et Orientalis 36 (Göttingen: Vandenhoeck & Ruprecht, 1981), for a critical evaluation of both the number and meaning of these readings.

68. Würthwein, *Text of the Old Testament*, 18.

69. Ibid., 19. Würthwein discusses, in addition to the *itture sopherim*, the occasions where the Hebrew Old Testament has only an unpointed word, i.e., only the consonants, in the text. This is referred to by the Masoretes as a reading that is "written, but not read." Alternately, there are occasions in which the Masoretic text will have vowels written in the text without any corresponding consonants. These cases are referred to as readings that are "read, but not written." Other authors limit the *itture sopherim* to only specialized cases. See next note.

70. Yeivin, *Tiberian Masorah*, 51, mentions that the *itture sopherim* refer to five passages where the conjunction *wāw* is to be omitted. Ginsburg, *Massoretico-Critical Edition*, 308–9, indicates that the five passages mentioned must be considered as only typical of a larger number. He lists at least eleven passages in the Pentateuch where the *wāw* should be omitted.

and the Masoretic notes. It will be convenient, however, to further distinguish between manuscripts that are dated before A.D. 1100 and those dated after A.D. 1100.

Manuscripts before A.D. 1100. Several of the first manuscripts to be considered actually date before A.D. 1000, but they are presented in this section because they basically represent the Tiberian Masoretic tradition in full bloom (see table 5).

TABLE 5   IMPORTANT MASORETIC MANUSCRIPTS

Name	Siglum	Date	Contents	Type/Comments
Aleppo Codex	A	925	all of OT, but most of Torah lost	pointed by Aaron ben Asher basis for Hebrew University Bible Project
Leningrad Codex	L	1008	all of OT	close to ben Asher tradition, but not as close as A basis for *BHK* 3d ed. and *BHS*
British Museum 4445	B	925	most of Torah	not as close to ben Asher as either A or L
Cairo Codex	C	896	Former and Latter Prophets	closer to ben Naphtali than ben Asher tradition
Sassoon 507	S	10th cent.	most of Torah	mixed text (ben Naphtali and ben Asher)
Sassoon 1053	S1	10th cent.	most of OT	least carefully written of group
Petersburg Codex	P	916	Latter Prophets	written with Babylonian vowel signs, but reflects Tiberian vowel tradition

The first of these is the Aleppo Codex (A), which dates from about A.D. 925.[71] According to an early colophon, the consonantal text was written by a scribe named Solomon ben Buyaa and the pointing, accents, and Masorah were written

71. Yeivin, *Tiberian Masorah*, 19.

by Aaron ben Asher himself.[72] The codex was thought to have been destroyed in 1948 in a period of anti-Jewish riots in Aleppo, but it was later discovered that a total of 294 out of an original 380 pages had been preserved. Today most of the Pentateuch is not extant.[73] The importance of this manuscript is its closeness to the ben Asher tradition and its use as the basis for a new critical edition of the Old Testament known as the Hebrew University Bible Project.[74]

The second manuscript of special note is the Leningrad Codex (L). This codex dates from A.D. 1008 and, though not as close to the ben Asher tradition as A, it is still very close. The differences between A and L have to do with certain vowel letters and the use of *metheg*.[75] The Leningrad Codex contains all of the Old Testament text and served as the basis for the third edition of the Hebrew Bible edited by Rudolf Kittel and the Stuttgart edition (*BHS*).[76]

A third important Old Testament manuscript is the British Museum MS Or. 4445 (B). This manuscript contains most of the Torah and, although lacking a colophon, it appears to date from about the time of A (ca. A.D. 925).[77] It is a fairly good representative of the ben Asher tradition, though not as close as either A or L. It may reflect a slightly earlier stage of Masoretic tradition than A.[78]

A fourth important manuscript is the Cairo Codex of the Prophets (C). Its colophon dates it ca. A.D. 896, and it is reputed to have been written by Moses ben Asher, the father of Aaron ben Asher.[79] The text contains all of the Prophets, and it is very carefully written. It appears to be closer to the ben

---

72. Ibid., 16.
73. Ibid., 17. Würthwein, *Text of the Old Testament*, 34, dates the Aleppo riots in 1947.
74. Cf. Moshe H. Goshen-Gottstein, *The Book of Isaiah: Sample Edition with Introduction* (Jerusalem: Magnes, 1965), 20.
75. Yeivin, *Tiberian Masorah*, 18–19. Würthwein, *Text of the Old Testament*, 168, indicates that the colophon allows for dates of A.D. 1010, 1009, or 1008. He concludes that 1008, derived from the rise of Islam, is best since the writer of the colophon lived in an Islamic country.
76. *BHS*, xi.
77. Yeivin, *Tiberian Masorah*, 19.
78. Ibid., 19–20.
79. Ibid., 20.

Naphtali tradition than to the ben Asher, though it is not a representative of a pure ben Naphtali text.[80]

Two early Tiberian manuscripts are both dated in more general terms to the tenth century A.D. The first of these is a manuscript of most of the Torah, formerly known as Sassoon 507 (S; now known as Jerusalem, National and University Library, Heb. 24° 5702). It is less closely aligned with the ben Asher tradition than the previously mentioned manuscripts, and in some instances it agrees with the ben Naphtali tradition.[81] The second contains the whole Old Testament except for a few missing pages, and is known as Sassoon 1053 (S¹). This manuscript is less carefully written than the others mentioned. The dot that distinguishes שׁ from שׂ is sometimes omitted.[82]

One additional manuscript should be mentioned for the sake of completeness: the Petersburg Codex of the Prophets (P). This manuscript contains the text of the Latter Prophets along with the Masorah *parva* and the Masorah *magna*. The special features of this text are its date (A.D. 916) and the character of its punctuation. The vowel pointing is represented by Babylonian signs, but the Masorah is Tiberian. A few pages of the codex show Tiberian pointing.[83]

Manuscripts after A.D. 1100. There are more than three thousand extant Hebrew manuscripts that reflect the Tiberian tradition and were written in the twelfth century and later. In the main, they do not differ greatly from the earlier manuscripts.[84] These manuscripts are termed "medieval," and they were the subject of study in the eighteenth century by Benjamin Kennicott and Johannes B. de Rossi.[85] Moshe Goshen-Gottstein's conclusion with respect to these manuscripts is that it is the "absence of [real variants] that marks medieval [manuscripts]."[86] The variants of these manuscripts indicate something about medieval scribal practices, but they

    80. Ibid.
    81. Ibid., 21.
    82. Ibid. There are many more manuscripts described in Yeivin's work than can be discussed here. For further details, see ibid., 22–29.
    83. Kahle, *Cairo Geniza*, 63.
    84. Würthwein, *Text of the Old Testament*, 39.
    85. Goshen-Gottstein, "Hebrew Biblical Manuscripts," 48–49.
    86. Ibid., 74.

do "not finally yield a single variant which is significantly, decisively, and undoubtedly connected with a pre-medieval tradition."[87]

The close of this phase of the history of the Old Testament text is marked by the invention of the printing press. The state of the Jewish transmission of the Old Testament text at the close of this period can be summarized as follows. The work of the Masoretes was concluded around A.D. 1000. This work, with some minor variations included, is represented in the important codexes that were described earlier. Between the twelfth century A.D. and the invention of the printing press, the main features of the Masoretic tradition were transmitted with very little change in the medieval Jewish manuscripts.

Textual Transmission from A.D. 1450 to the Present

The last phase of the history of the Jewish transmission of the text begins with the appearance of printed Hebrew Bibles (or printed portions of the Old Testament) in the late fifteenth century A.D. The earliest printed exemplars of the Old Testament include the Psalms (1477 in Bologna?), the Prophets (1485–86 in Soncino), the Writings (1486–87 in Naples), and the Pentateuch (1491 in Lisbon).[88] The first complete printed Hebrew Bibles were published in Soncino (1488), Naples (1491–93), and Brescia (1494).[89] By the sixteenth century A.D. printed editions replaced manuscripts in most of Europe. Only in areas without printing facilities did manuscript copying continue to be practiced. In Yemen, hand copying of the Old Testament text continued down to modern times.[90]

A major development came somewhat later with the publication of the so-called Rabbinic Bibles. The first Rabbinic Bible was edited by Felix Pratensis and published by Daniel Bomberg in 1516–17.[91] Of even greater importance was the second Rabbinic Bible that was edited by Jacob ben Hayyim ben Adoniyahu and printed by Daniel Bomberg (A.D. 1524–25

87. Ibid., 77.
88. Würthwein, *Text of the Old Testament*, 37.
89. Ibid.
90. Yeivin, *Tiberian Masorah*, 31.
91. Würthwein, *Text of the Old Testament*, 37.

in Venice). This second Rabbinic Bible, like its predecessor, contained the Hebrew text with vowels, the accents, and the Masorah (small, large, and final). It also contained Aramaic Targums and some Jewish commentaries by outstanding rabbis such as Rashi, Ibn Ezra, and David Qimḥi.[92] Apparently ben Hayyim used manuscripts from the twelfth century and later.[93] The Bomberg edition came to be known as the "Received Edition," and it was copied in many succeeding editions of Rabbinic Bibles.[94] The Bomberg (or ben Hayyim) edition was also used as the basis for the first and second editions of the Kittel Bible.[95]

There were several printed editions in the eighteenth to early twentieth centuries. Among these may be mentioned an edition of Michaelis (Halle, 1720), an edition by Seligmann Baer and Friedrich Delitzsch (late 1800s), and the edition of Christian D. Ginsburg (early 1900s). Ginsburg's edition was substantially the text of ben Hayyim along with variants found in manuscripts and editions dating before 1524.[96]

As mentioned earlier, the first two editions of Kittel's Old Testament printed the ben Hayyim text. It was not until the third edition that the ben Hayyim text was replaced with the text of the Leningrad Codex.[97] Another edition was prepared for the British and Foreign Bible Society by Norman H. Snaith in 1958. Snaith used three manuscripts: primarily British Museum MS Or. 2626–2628 (written in Lisbon in 1482), but also British Museum MS Or. 2375 (a Yemenite manuscript dating from 1468–1480) and the Shem Tob manuscript (a Spanish manuscript dated 1312). These manuscripts are all quite close to the ben Asher text, so Snaith's edition is quite close to the third edition of the Kittel Bible.[98]

The most recent editions for the critical study of the Old Testament are the *Biblia Hebraica Stuttgartensia* (*BHS*) and

92. Yeivin, *Tiberian Masorah*, 31; Würthwein, *Text of the Old Testament*, 37.
93. Yeivin, *Tiberian Masorah*, 31.
94. Ibid., 31–32.
95. Würthwein, *Text of the Old Testament*, 37.
96. Ibid., 39.
97. *BHK*, xxvi.
98. Würthwein, *Text of the Old Testament*, 40.

the edition that is being prepared by the Hebrew University Bible Project. The Stuttgart edition was first published in fascicles, beginning in 1968, and the complete edition was published in 1977.[99] The Hebrew University Bible Project has published a sample from the Book of Isaiah (1965) and the first two parts of the Book of Isaiah (1975–81).[100]

Conclusion

The history of the transmission of the Old Testament text is long and involved (see table 6). The important features of that

TABLE 6   HEBREW TRANSMISSION OF THE OLD TESTAMENT

prior to 300 B.C.	individual books written and copied on scrolls revision of Hebrew grammar (after 1350 B.C.) introduction of some vowel letters (spelling changes) occasional crowding sometimes mars word division change from archaic script to square script
from 300 B.C. to A.D. 135	development of text types adoption of proto-Masoretic Text

from A.D. 135 to A.D. 1000	Talmudic period:
	    book form for private copies; scrolls for synagogues
	    verse, paragraph, and liturgical divisions
	    avoidance of indelicate expressions
	Masoretic period:
	    written vowel system
	    accent system
	    Masoretic notes
	    Kethiv-Qere finalized
	    separate Masoretic treatises
	    tiqqune sopherim finalized (?)

from A.D. 1000 to A.D. 1450	transmission of the Masoretic Text (with only *minor* changes)
from A.D. 1450 to present	invention of the printing press printed editions modern critical editions

99. *BHS*, iii.
100. Cf., e.g., Goshen-Gottstein, *Book of Isaiah*.

history have now been traced from the time of the first writing of individual books up to the critical editions available or becoming available at the present time. When the vast amount of time that separates our modern editions from the autographs is considered, especially in view of the need for hand copying for much of that time, it is amazing that we have *any* Old Testament. It is even more amazing that we have access to a generally faithful copy of the Old Testament that is substantially the same as the autographs written so many years ago. Obviously, there are places in the Old Testament where the text may be in doubt, and in places the testimony of the ancient versions will be necessary to restore the text. But by and large, the Hebrew text that we have has been faithfully (though not perfectly) transmitted down through the years.[101] The story of the ancient versions of the Old Testament text will be the topic of the following chapter.

101. Talmon, "Old Testament Text," 166, speaks of the difference in the period beginning early in the third century B.C. between the copying of the Old Testament books and the copying of noncanonical books: "We have no reason to suppose that much heed was paid to the text of non-sanctified writings, nor does the traceable textual history of writings of this kind, such as Ecclesiasticus, substantiate such an assumption. Since they had no claim to have been conceived under divine inspiration, variants in their transmitted wordings were regarded as of no consequence."

3

Ancient Versions
of the Old Testament

The previous chapter described the history of the transmission of the complete text of the Old Testament in Hebrew. The present chapter deals with its transmission in a variety of languages other than Hebrew.[1] In each case, the treatment includes three basic kinds of information. First, there is a historical survey of the origin of the Old Testament text in the dress of a specific linguistic medium. Second, the general character of the text form transmitted in a given language is described. And finally, a general evaluation of the usefulness of the particular linguistic tradition for Old Testament textual criticism is included. The Samaritan Pentateuch is discussed first because it is most closely related to the Hebrew Old Testament manuscripts.[2] The Aramaic Targums are discussed in second place because they are less distant, in a linguistic

1. The Samaritan Pentateuch is included in this chapter even though it transmits the text in Hebrew. See the following discussion and especially note 2.

2. The Samaritan Pentateuch is not, to be precisely accurate, a version. Cf. Ernst Würthwein, *The Text of the Old Testament*, trans. Erroll F. Rhodes (Grand Rapids: Eerdmans, 1979), 42–44. It is included with the versions for practical reasons. The Samaritans did not preserve the entire Old Testament text as their Scripture. Additionally, the Samaritan transmission of the Pentateuch was basically separate from mainstream Jewish text transmission from about 100 B.C. (see references in note 4). For the basis of locating the Samaritan Pentateuch with the versions, see Shemaryahu Talmon, "The Samaritan Pentateuch," *Journal of Jewish Studies* 2 (1950–51): 149, who notes that "in this respect [the Samaritan Pentateuch] falls in line with those translations, in the sense that it is a popular edition of the Pentateuch in the Hebrew language."

sense, from the Hebrew text than are other versions of the Old Testament. The Greek versions are considered next because of their great importance as witnesses to the Old Testament Scriptures. Finally, several other versions of the Old Testament are mentioned in order to give a more complete picture of Old Testament textual history.

Samaritan Pentateuch

As the name implies, the Samaritan Pentateuch contains only the Pentateuch (Torah) as it was preserved by the Samaritan community. The Samaritans were a mixed group whose origin may be traced to the time of the captivity of the northern kingdom of Israel.[3] As a group, they recognized only the Pentateuch, or Torah, as their authoritative (canonical) Scripture. Therefore it is the only portion of the Old Testament that they copied and preserved throughout their history.[4]

The Samaritans preserved their Pentateuch in an archaic script that is a derivative of the Phoenician–paleo-Hebrew script.[5] This contrasts with the Old Testament preserved by the Jews, which was first written and copied in the archaic script, but later came to be preserved in the square, or Aramaic, script. Early Samaritan manuscripts would have been

3. The origins of the Samaritan people, according to the Old Testament, are given in 2 Kings 17. In the postexilic era, the Samaritans and Jews were hostile to one another (cf. the books of Ezra and Nehemiah), a hostility that was also very much in evidence in the time of Jesus. Jews would take a long detour to avoid traveling through Samaria (John 4).

4. At one point it was customary to date the Samaritan schism to the fourth century B.C. That the Samaritans accepted only the Pentateuch as Scripture was seen as evidence that the Pentateuch was the only part of the Old Testament that had attained canonical status at the time of the schism. Recent studies have shown that the Samaritan schism is to be dated toward the end of the second century B.C. The existence of the Samaritan Pentateuch thus contributes nothing to the question of the canon of the Old Testament. Cf. James D. Purvis, *The Samaritan Pentateuch and the Origin of the Samaritan Sect* (Cambridge: Harvard University Press, 1968), 14, 16, 113–118; and Roger T. Beckwith, *The Old Testament Canon of the New Testament Church and Its Background in Early Judaism* (Grand Rapids: Eerdmans, 1985), 6.

5. Würthwein, *Text of the Old Testament*, 4–6.

purely consonantal (unvocalized), but some manuscripts of the twelfth century A.D. and later have a partial vocalization that is very similar to the Palestinian system of vocalizing Hebrew texts.[6]

The existence of the Samaritan Pentateuch first became known in the West when a manuscript was discovered in Damascus in A.D. 1616 by Pietro della Valle.[7] In 1631 John Morinus judged the Samaritan Pentateuch to be much better than the Masoretic Text. The text discovered by della Valle was subsequently published in both the Paris Polyglot (1645) and the London Polyglot (1657).[8] In 1815 Wilhelm Gesenius published his classic study of the Samaritan Pentateuch. Based on both the history and character of the text, he concluded that the Samaritan Pentateuch had no value for recovering the original text of the Old Testament. His views carried the day for the rest of the nineteenth century.[9] In 1915 Paul Kahle argued for a more positive evaluation of the Samaritan Pentateuch and accepted more of its readings as genuine than had Gesenius. His conclusions were based in part on the witness to the Samaritan text that is found in certain apocryphal books, the Septuagint, and the New Testament.[10] With the discovery of the Qumran scrolls the understanding of the place and value of the Samaritan Pentateuch became even clearer. Some Qumran documents are similar in many respects to the text form of the Samaritan Pentateuch. (See the discussion in chapter 2 for Cross's explanation of the relation

6. Paul E. Kahle, *The Cairo Geniza*, 2d ed. (Oxford: Blackwell, 1959), 66. Emanuel Tov, *Textual Criticism of the Hebrew Bible* (Minneapolis: Fortress, 1992), 81, indicates that ancient Samaritan manuscripts were rarely and inconsistently vocalized. Only recently have Samaritans provided fully vocalized manuscripts for those outside their own religious community.

7. Würthwein, *Text of the Old Testament*, 42; see also Frederic Kenyon, *Our Bible and the Ancient Manuscripts* (New York: Harper, 1941), 49–50.

8. Bruce K. Waltke, "Samaritan Pentateuch," in *The Anchor Bible Dictionary*, ed. David N. Freedman et al. (New York: Doubleday, 1992), 5:932. Concerning the whole question of the Samaritan Pentateuch, note also, Waltke's "The Samaritan Pentateuch and the Text of the Old Testament," in *New Perspectives on the Old Testament*, ed. J. Barton Payne (Waco: Word, 1970), 212–39.

9. Waltke, "Samaritan Pentateuch" (*ABD*), 932.

10. Ibid., 933.

between the various forms of the Old Testament text by means of his theory of local texts.)

The text of the Samaritan Pentateuch is currently available for study in a variety of manuscripts, printed editions, and translations. The manuscript discovered by della Valle, as already mentioned, was printed as part of the Paris and London polyglots. It is also represented in Blayney's edition (1790) and in August F. von Gall's critical and eclectic text (1918). The latter, because of the principles used to prepare it, must be used with caution.[11] The *Sefer Abisha* scroll, some parts of which are to be dated to A.D. 1149, is the basis of two more recent editions of the Samaritan Pentateuch: the edition of the scroll by Federico Pérez Castro (1959) and an edition supplemented by another manuscript and edited by Sadaqa (1962–65).[12] A codex from A.D. 1100, along with variants from fifteen unpublished manuscripts, has been published by L. F. Giron-Blanc (1976).[13]

In addition to the various Samaritan manuscripts and editions written in Hebrew, there are translations that also witness to the text of the Samaritan Pentateuch. These witnesses include a Greek translation (the Samaritikon), an Aramaic version (a Samaritan Targum), and an Arabic translation. The Greek translation, mentioned by Origen in the Hexapla, exists only in fragmentary form (Deut. 24–29). The Samaritan Targum, written in a dialect of West Aramaic, is extremely difficult to use due to the faulty understanding of Hebrew of its translator(s) and the ignorance of Aramaic of the scribes who copied it.[14] According to Kahle, the Samaritan Targum never existed in the form of a *textus receptus*.[15] The Samaritans in the eleventh century A.D. initially used Saadia Gaon's Arabic translation of the Old Testament (Pentateuch). Soon afterward, they began to adapt this translation to the text of the Samaritan Pentateuch. Later, in the second half of the thirteenth century, Abu Said revised the translation(s) and

11. Ibid., 935.
12. Ibid.
13. Ibid.
14. Ibid.
15. Kahle, *Cairo Geniza*, 52.

produced a text that became a recognized Arabic version (a *textus receptus*) for the Samaritans.[16] The overall character of the Samaritan Pentateuch can be perceived by noting that it differs from the Masoretic Text of the Pentateuch some six thousand times. The Septuagint agrees with the Samaritan Pentateuch against the Masoretic text in about nineteen hundred cases.[17] This needs qualification, however, or the text critic may seriously misunderstand the situation.[18] Bruce Waltke summarizes the character of the Samaritan Pentateuch under eight headings. His first category includes the kinds of scribal errors that are normal in the manual transmission of any ancient text. These errors could be termed the result of inner-Samaritan textual corruption. The second class of readings in the Samaritan Pentateuch reflect a different grammar than what became normative for the Masoretic Text. Another type of variant relates to modernizations of archaic forms. A fourth category of change within the Samaritan Pentateuch is the removal of grammatical difficulties. These include a more consistent orthography (spelling) as well as a more consistent matching of number and gender between subjects and verbs. Another type of difference in the Samaritan text includes both the addition of a word (or words) to clarify the meaning of a text and the inclusion of a shorter or longer addition from a parallel passage. A sixth class of variation attempts to make the text more consistent historically. A seventh category of small changes interpret and clarify the text. The final kind of change in the Samaritan Pentateuch is that motivated by Samaritan theology.[19] An example of this last category of read-

16. Ibid., 54–55.
17. Würthwein, *Text of the Old Testament*, 43. Some authors, e.g., Ralph W. Klein, *Textual Criticism of the Old Testament* (Philadelphia: Fortress, 1974), 17, give a somewhat different number (about 1,600) for the agreements between the Samaritan Pentateuch and the Septuagint. Waltke, "Samaritan Pentateuch" (*ABD*), 932, indicates that this collation of variants between the Samaritan Pentateuch, Septuagint, and Masoretic Text goes back to work done by Cassellus in the mid-seventeenth century A.D.
18. Purvis, *Samaritan Pentateuch*, 70, states that the total text of the Samaritan Pentateuch is actually closer to the Masoretic Text than it is to the Septuagint.
19. Waltke, "Samaritan Pentateuch" (*ABD*), 936–38.

ing is the possible substitution of Mount Gerizim for Mount Ebal in Deuteronomy 27:4. This (altered) text is also inserted in the Ten Commandments in Exodus 20 and Deuteronomy 5, thus indicating that God commanded that Mount Gerizim was the place where he was to be worshiped.[20] Another intentional change is the repeated alteration throughout the Book of Deuteronomy of the phrase *the place Yahweh will choose* (MT) to *the place Yahweh chose* (SP).

The value of the Samaritan Pentateuch for Old Testament textual criticism is related to the preceding description of its textual character. Although it was once viewed as superior to the Masoretic Text, most text critics today do not hold this view. There are four reasons for this judgment. First, the Samaritan Pentateuch probably reflects a popular text form of the Old Testament, not the strict form that was transmitted by the Jews.[21] Second, the standard critical edition of the Samaritan Pentateuch must be used with caution: It "is based on questionable canons of criticisms . . . , and it contains errors, relies too heavily on the MT, and lacks important sources such as the ʾAbishaᶜ Scroll."[22] Third, the Samaritan Pentateuch is less important because there is less need for textual criticism in the Pentateuch than in other parts of the Old Testament. Finally, there is no copy of the Samaritan Pentateuch that is older than the tenth century A.D. This further reduces its overall value for textual criticism.[23]

The preceding characterization of the Samaritan Pentateuch does not mean it has no place in Old Testament textual criticism (the position developed by Gesenius). Samaritan readings, where they differ from the Masoretic Text, need

---

20. Robert H. Pfeiffer, *Introduction to the Old Testament* (New York: Harper, 1941), 102; cf. also Artur Weiser, *The Old Testament: Its Formation and Development*, trans. Dorothea M. Barton (New York: Association Press/ London: Darton, Longman & Todd, 1961), 367.

21. Würthwein, *Text of the Old Testament*, 43.

22. Waltke, "Samaritan Pentateuch" (*ABD*), 935. The standard critical edition by August F. von Gall was first published in 1918 and reprinted in 1966; cf. James D. Purvis, "Samaritan Pentateuch," in *The Interpreter's Dictionary of the Bible: Supplementary Volume*, ed. Keith Crim (Nashville: Abingdon, 1976), 774.

23. Kenyon, *Our Bible and the Ancient Manuscripts*, 52.

to be considered on a case-by-case basis. In some instances the Samaritan reading preserves the original text. What should be maintained is that the Samaritan Pentateuch does not serve for any wholesale setting aside of the Masoretic Text of the Pentateuch (see figure 2).

FIGURE 2   SAMARITAN PENTATEUCH

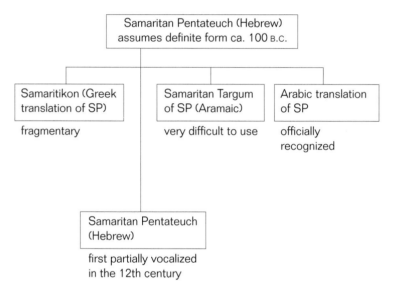

Targums

The Targums are Aramaic translations of certain books or larger sections of the Old Testament.[24] As a general rule, Targums tend to be more paraphrastic than literal. They owe their origin to the time when Hebrew fell out of common use among the Jewish people in Palestine.[25] Because the ordinary Jew came to speak Aramaic instead of Hebrew, synagogue readings had to be given in Aramaic to be understood. At first

24. The standard critical edition of the official Targums to the Pentateuch and the Prophets is Alexander Sperber, *The Bible in Aramaic*, 4 vols. (Leiden: Brill, 1959–73).

25. Sperber, *Bible in Aramaic*, 4B:1.

this was done orally, but in time these translations came to be written down.[26] Several different Targums are known today. The most important of these are the official Targums. Targum Onqelos (also spelled Onkelos) is the official Targum of the Pentateuch. Within the overall Targum tradition it represents a rather literal translation of the Hebrew text. There is some tendency to paraphrase, but there is also indication of curtailed paraphrase (i.e., paraphrase removed through an editing process). Onqelos was probably reduced to writing in the second century A.D., but its text rests on pre-Christian traditions. It may have undergone an editing process in the fourth or fifth century A.D. in Babylon.[27] Additional features of Onqelos are the removal of some anthropomorphisms, a tendency toward idealization of the patriarchs, and the replacement of archaic names with more modern forms.[28]

Targum Jonathan, like Targum Onqelos, is an official Targum that was recognized and accepted by Judaism. Like Onqelos it originated in Palestine, but was later redacted in Babylonia. It was cited as authoritative in the Babylonian Talmud at the beginning of the fourth century A.D. Targum Jonathan contains the prophetic books of the Old Testament, both Early Prophets (Joshua, Judges, Samuel, and Kings) and Latter Prophets (the Major Prophets, minus Daniel, and the Minor Prophets). Targum Jonathan is generally more paraphrastic than Targum Onqelos, and this feature is more pronounced in the Latter Prophets, especially in the Targum to Isaiah.[29]

26. Würthwein, *Text of the Old Testament*, 75; and Martin McNamara, "Targums," in *The Interpreter's Dictionary of the Bible: Supplementary Volume*, ed. Keith Crim (Nashville: Abingdon, 1976), 860. Note that Jewish tradition associates the beginnings of this process of giving an oral rendering of the Hebrew Scriptures with the time of Ezra in the postexilic community (Neh. 8:8).

27. Martin McNamara, *Targum and Testament* (Grand Rapids: Eerdmans, 1972), 173–75.

28. Aage Bentzen, *Introduction to the Old Testament* (Copenhagen: Gad, 1948), 1:69.

29. McNamara, *Targum and Testament*, 206–7. A new series in the process of publication, "The Aramaic Bible," edited by Kevin Cathcart, Michael Maher, and Martin McNamara, offers an English translation, introduction, and notes for the official Targums of the Old Testament.

The Cairo Geniza provided additional information about an earlier stage of Targum production. Fragments of a Palestinian Targum were discovered among other Geniza materials. These fragments give evidence of the existence of a complete Targum of the Pentateuch that was once highly esteemed. The Palestinian Targum may be related to an original Targum that, after editorial activity in Babylon, came to be officially recognized as Targum Onqelos.[30] In 1956 Alejandro Díez Macho discovered an almost complete text of a Palestinian Targum of the Pentateuch in Codex Neofiti I of the Vatican Library. This Targum was apparently copied in A.D. 1504. An *editio princeps* of this Targum with accompanying introductory material and appendices was published between 1968 and 1979.[31]

Other unofficial Targums to the Pentateuch are Targum Pseudo-Jonathan (also known as Targum Yerushalmi I) and the "Fragmentary Targum" (or Fragment-Targum).[32] Targum Pseudo-Jonathan must not be confused with Targum Jonathan to the Prophets (described above). Both Targum Pseudo-Jonathan and the Fragmentary Targum are considered Palestinian Targums, but they are transitional between the early Palestinian Targum and the later Jewish official Targums. All books in the Hebrew Bible have at least one Targum, except Daniel and Ezra–Nehemiah. All of these, except possibly Proverbs, are written in Palestinian Aramaic.[33] The Targums to various books of the Writ-

30. Bleddyn J. Roberts, *The Old Testament Text and Versions* (Cardiff: University of Wales Press, 1951), 200.

31. Alejandro Díez Macho (ed.), *Neophyti I: Targum Palestinense MS de la Bibliotheca Vaticana*, 6 vols. (Madrid: Consejo Superior de Investigaciones Científicas, 1968–79).

32. The Fragment-Targum must not be confused with the fragments of Targum material that were found in the Cairo Geniza. The Geniza fragments were apparently fragments, often several chapters long, of complete Targums that survived by chance. The Fragment-Targums (the more appropriate phrase) are fragmentary collections of Targum material. Most often these collections contain a series of isolated verses, parts of verses, or even isolated words. Full documentation can be found in Michael L. Klein, *The Fragment-Targums of the Pentateuch according to Their Extant Sources*, 2 vols., Analecta Biblica 76 (Rome: Pontifical Biblical Institute Press, 1980).

33. McNamara, *Targum and Testament*, 209.

ings vary greatly among themselves. For example, the Targum to the Psalms is a mixture of strict literalism and extreme paraphrase. The Targums to the five Megilloth are extremely paraphrastic.[34] The value of the Targums for textual criticism of the Old Testament is less than might be expected, primarily due to the historical background of their original production as oral paraphrases. As paraphrases, aimed at the understanding of the Jewish worshipers, they are of more value as examples of Jewish homiletical procedures and trends than as precise instruments of textual transmission.[35] This does not mean that no Targum can ever aid in the determination of the original text of the Old Testament. It merely indicates the general character and overall usefulness of the Targums in the study of the Old Testament text (see table 7).[36]

TABLE 7   TARGUMS OF THE OLD TESTAMENT

Pentateuch	Targum Onqelos (Official)
	Codex Neofiti I (Palestinian)
	Targum Pseudo-Jonathan (Palestinian)
	Fragment-Targum (Palestinian)
	Fragments of Palestinian Targum in Cairo Geniza
Prophets	Targum Jonathan (Official)
Writings	Various unofficial Targums available except for Daniel and Ezra–Nehemiah

Greek Versions

Pride of place among the non-Semitic ancient versions of the Old Testament must be granted to the Septuagint and to its

34. Roberts, *Old Testament Text*, 209–10. Cf. also Sperber, *Bible in Aramaic*, 4A:v, who introduces the Targum to Esther with the title "Targum a Misnomer for Midrash."

35. Würthwein, *Text of the Old Testament*, 76.

36. Roberts, *Old Testament Text*, 211, states that the Targums generally do not give any help in discovering textual corruption in the Old Testament except when they confirm the variants of other versions.

many revisions and recensions.[37] There are four reasons for this special importance. First, the Septuagint was initially translated in the third to second centuries B.C. It thus represents the earliest of the translations of the Old Testament. Second, the Septuagint is well attested by large numbers of ancient manuscripts, several of which are very old. Third, the Septuagint contains the entire text of the Old Testament. What was partial in the case of both the Samaritan Pentateuch and the official Targums is complete in the case of the Septuagint.[38] And finally, the Septuagint is important for textual criticism of the Old Testament because it reflects more important variants than all other textual witnesses combined.[39]

The infamous Letter of Aristeas explains in great detail how the Greek Old Testament came to be, but many of the details are undoubtedly apocryphal. Nevertheless, certain historical facts may be gleaned from the letter. These include the location (Alexandria, Egypt), the time (during the reign of Ptolemy Philadelphus, 285–246 B.C.), the initial extent (the Pentateuch), the parties involved (the Jews), and the nature of the effort (an officially sanctioned effort aimed at synagogue worship and instruction).[40] Other Old Testament books were undoubtedly translated at a somewhat later time, with the entire process completed no later than 150 B.C.[41]

37. The name *Septuagint* derives from the tradition that 70 (or 72) individuals produced the translation. The two standard editions, neither complete, are Alan E. Brooke, Norman McLean, and Henry St. J. Thackeray (eds.), *The Old Testament in Greek* (Cambridge: Cambridge University Press, 1906–40), based on the text of Vaticanus, and *Septuaginta* (Göttingen: Vandenhoeck & Ruprecht, 1931–), based on an eclectic text. The Cambridge edition ceased publication in 1940, but the Göttingen edition is ongoing. Cf. Sidney Jellicoe, *The Septuagint and Modern Study* (Oxford: Clarendon, 1968; reprinted Ann Arbor, Mich.: Eisenbrauns, 1978), 18–23.

38. Kenyon, *Our Bible and the Ancient Manuscripts*, 52.

39. Emanuel Tov, *The Text-Critical Use of the Septuagint in Biblical Research* (Jerusalem: Simor, 1981), 272.

40. Jellicoe, *Septuagint and Modern Study*, 55–56. Tov, *Text-Critical Use of the Septuagint*, 254, disputes the claim that all parts of the Septuagint reflect an Egyptian provenance. Given that parts of the current Septuagint may not have been produced in Egypt, it still seems that a general recognition of the Egyptian origin of most of the Septuagint is a valid historical conclusion.

41. Cf. Würthwein, *Text of the Old Testament*, 51. The prologue to Sirach (Ecclesiasticus), written ca. 116 B.C., mentions the Greek translation of "the

The Greek Old Testament was thus initially produced by Jews. Between the original production of the Septuagint[42] and the Greek versions of the second century A.D. there were two early revisions. The earlier is called "proto-Lucian" because it shares characteristics with the fourth-century A.D. revision of Lucian. It is to be dated sometime in the first century B.C. It is designated as *proto*-Lucian because some of the readings it shares with the later Lucianic recension are reflected in both Josephus (first century A.D.) and the Old Latin translation (second century A.D.).[43] According to Cross, proto-Lucian represents a sporadic correction of the Old Greek (i.e., the original Septuagint) toward the Palestinian textual family that is represented by the three Samuel texts found at Qumran.[44]

The later of these early revisions is called the *kaige* recension for its characteristic translation of the Hebrew word םג (*gam*) by the Greek word καίγε (*kaige*). It dates to the late first century B.C. or the early first century A.D., and its overall character is seen as a revision of the Old Greek translation in the direction of conformity with the proto-Masoretic Text.[45] The *kaige* recension exerted some influence on all three of the second-century A.D. revisions of the Greek Old Testament.

In time the Septuagint came to be adopted by the Christian

Law itself, the Prophecies, and the rest of the books" (New Revised Standard Version) as a well-known document.

42. Scholars dispute the legitimacy of referring to *the* original Septuagint. Some prefer to speak of a variety of early Greek translations that in time coalesced into a uniform tradition. The discussion is beyond the scope of this book, but details may be found in Würthwein, *Text of the Old Testament*, 59–63.

43. Klein, *Textual Criticism*, 23.

44. Frank M. Cross, "The Evolution of a Theory of Local Texts," in *Qumran and the History of the Biblical Text*, ed. Frank M. Cross and Shemaryahu Talmon (Cambridge: Harvard University Press, 1975), 312.

45. Klein, *Textual Criticism*, 23–24. Jellicoe, *Septuagint and Modern Study*, 83, dates the *kaige* (or *Ur*-Theodotion) recension to the early part of the first century B.C. Cf. Cross, "Theory of Local Texts," 313, for the link to the proto-Masoretic Text. The *kaige* recension is called "R" by Dominique Barthélemy, "Redécouverte d'un Chainon Manquant de l'Histoire de la Septante," in *Qumran and the History of the Biblical Text*, ed. Frank M. Cross and Shemaryahu Talmon (Cambridge: Harvard University Press, 1975), 132.

churches. Since it was often used in debates between Christians and Jews, it came to be viewed with suspicion by the latter. This led, in the course of the second century A.D., to the production of three rival Greek versions that each bore a different relationship to the original Septuagint.[46] The earliest of these rival versions (ca. A.D. 150) was produced by Aquila, a Jewish proselyte and disciple of Rabbi Akiva.[47] The most noteworthy characteristic of Aquila's version is its extreme literalness. Sidney Jellicoe suggests that it was never intended for popular circulation, but that it was to be a teacher's book that gave an exact rendering of the Hebrew text.[48] Dominique Barthélemy argues that Aquila adopted the principal ideas of the *kaige* recension and refined them to the point of perfection.[49]

The second rival version of the second century A.D. was produced by Theodotion. His work is somewhat later than Aquila's, and his Greek is much more free than Aquila's stilted literalness. His religious affiliation is in doubt, but his version became very popular with the Christian church. His rendering of Daniel even came to replace the original Septuagint translation in the church's Old Testament.[50]

Actually, the relationship between LXX-Daniel and Theodotion-Daniel is more complicated. Alexander Di Lella argues that the translation known as Theodotion-Daniel is not related

46. Würthwein, *Text of the Old Testament*, 53. Note that some writers speak of these productions as new translations (e.g., Kenyon, *Our Bible and the Ancient Manuscripts*, 56); others refer to them as "revisions" (e.g., Jellicoe, *Septuagint and Modern Study*, 74). The problem relates in part to the existence of readings that are characteristic of, say, Aquila, but also are found outside of and *before* Aquila.

47. Kenyon, *Our Bible and the Ancient Manuscripts*, 56.

48. Jellicoe, *Septuagint and Modern Study*, 77, 80.

49. Dominique Barthélemy, *Les Devanciers d'Aquila*, Vetus Testamentum Supplement 10 (Leiden: Brill, 1963), xi, 81–88.

50. Kenyon, *Our Bible and the Ancient Manuscripts*, 56–57; Jellicoe, *Septuagint and Modern Study*, 83–84. Note that in Joseph Ziegler (ed.), *Susanna, Daniel, Bel et Draco*, Göttingen Septuagint 16/2 (Göttingen: Vandenhoeck & Ruprecht, 1954), the text of Theodotion-Daniel is printed on the top of each page while the Hexaplaric text is printed at the bottom. Alfred Rahlfs's edition (*Septuaginta* [Stuttgart: Württembergische Bibelanstalt, 1935]) of the Septuagint also prints the two translations of Daniel, but in this case the Hexaplaric text is at the top and the Theodotionic text is at the bottom.

to either proto(*Ur*)-Theodotion or the traditional (second century A.D.) Theodotion. According to Di Lella this latter point is required because the New Testament quotes from Theodotion-Daniel in various places. Di Lella sees Theodotion-Daniel as a fresh translation of the Hebrew-Aramaic portions of the original book with some knowledge of LXX-Daniel.[51]

The last of the rival second-century A.D. versions was produced by Symmachus in the closing years of the century. Symmachus was the most gifted of these three individuals, at least in terms of Greek style, and he produced a very popular translation that has been described as "idiomatic Greek, [though] tending to paraphrase."[52] As an interesting sidelight, the version of Symmachus had little impact on the subsequent history of the transmission of the Septuagint, but it did exert quite an influence on Jerome and the Latin Vulgate.[53]

The next major stage in the history of the Greek Old Testament was a logical one given the preceding history. At the end of the second century there were (at least) four competing Greek versions of the Old Testament. The discrepancies between these four versions and their differences with respect to the Hebrew text were bewildering, to say the least. It was at this point in history that a very special individual came to center stage, a man named Origen. He was a native of Egypt, but later on he settled in Caesarea. He set out to bring order and understanding to the confusing array of competing textual witnesses to the Old Testament text. His work resulted in the massive volume known as the Hexapla. This work, when originally completed, ran to some 6,500 pages and took some fifteen years to complete.[54]

---

51. Louis F. Hartman and Alexander A. Di Lella, *Daniel*, Anchor Bible 23 (Garden City, N.Y.: Doubleday, 1978), 81–82.

52. Henry St. John Thackeray, *A Grammar of the Old Testament in Greek* (Cambridge: Cambridge University Press, 1909), 5. In his *Septuagint and Jewish Worship*, Schweich Lectures 1920 (Oxford: Oxford University Press for the British Academy, 1923), 14, Thackeray further describes the style of Symmachus as "elegant . . . read[ing] like a direct challenge to Aquila's monstrosities."

53. Kenyon, *Our Bible and the Ancient Manuscripts*, 57.

54. Jellicoe, *Septuagint and Modern Study*, 101.

The Hexapla was a six-column work in which the existing Greek versions could be compared with the Hebrew text that was current in Origen's time. The arrangement was as follows. The first column was the Hebrew text. The second column was a transliteration of the Hebrew text in Greek letters. The third column contained Aquila's version, the fourth Symmachus's, the fifth Origen's own revision of the Septuagint text, and the final column Theodotion's version. The fifth column originally had a series of special symbols that indicated whether material had been added or deleted in order to make it match the Hebrew text.[55]

Due to the magnitude of Origen's work, it was probably never copied in its entirety.[56] The fifth column was much copied in subsequent years, but often with no regard for the special symbols that Origen had used. Since the fifth column was actually Origen's own revision, he unwittingly added to the textual confusion that he had aimed to resolve. There was, however, one specific rendering of Origen's fifth column that carefully included his special symbols. This is the translation of Origen's fifth column into Syriac by Paul of Tella in A.D. 616–617.[57] Through this vehicle much of Origen's work of revising the Septuagint can be recovered and appreciated.

Two additional individuals left a mark on early Septuagintal history: Lucian and Hesychius. Lucian was a presbyter of Antioch who was martyred in ca. A.D. 311. The peculiarity of his work on the Greek Old Testament is a tendency to conflation (i.e., a combining of two variant readings into a single reading).[58] Hesychius, who may well be the martyred bishop of the same name, produced a Greek version ca. A.D. 300, which is reflected in part in Codex Vaticanus.[59]

---

55. There were also other columns mentioned for certain Old Testament books. These are referred to as the *Quinta* (as following the fourth Greek column), *Sexta*, and *Septima*; cf. Klein, *Textual Criticism*, 7.

56. Würthwein, *Text of the Old Testament*, 57.

57. Ibid. This translation of Origen's fifth column was called the Syro-Hexapla to distinguish it from the Peshitta Version of the Old Testament in Syriac.

58. Kenyon, *Our Bible and the Ancient Manuscripts*, 60; Jellicoe, *Septuagint and Modern Study*, 159.

59. Jellicoe, *Septuagint and Modern Study*, 153.

Recovering the original Septuagint text is complicated by the mixed nature of the uncial manuscripts (i.e., there is no single uncial that exclusively reflects any of the three editions of the early fourth century A.D.).[60] The major task of Septuagint research today is to move from the great uncial manuscripts (primarily Vaticanus, Sinaiticus, and Alexandrinus) back to the texts of Origen, Lucian, and Hesychius. Once these texts have been established, attempts can be made to penetrate even further back until the original text of the Septuagint is established. Two major efforts, neither of which is complete at present, are aimed at accomplishing this task: the Cambridge and Göttingen Septuagint projects. The Cambridge edition, now defunct, uses the text of Vaticanus as a base text. Where this text is lacking, the text of Alexandrinus or other uncials is used. Minor variants are included in the apparatus immediately below the text. Substantive variant readings found in other uncials, selected cursives, important ancient versions, and early ecclesiastical writers are given in the main apparatus. No attempt is made in the Cambridge edition "to provide a reconstructed or 'true' Septuagint text."[61] The goal is to provide a "trustworthy collection of textual material" that will allow the user to attempt to reconstruct the original Septuagint text.[62] The Göttingen edition (incomplete, but still in production) offers a reconstructed (eclectic) text as a base, and includes variant readings in two separate textual apparatuses.[63]

Certain general principles can be stated at this point in our discussion relative to the use of the Septuagint in Old Testament textual criticism. First, as has been indicated above, the initial task is to carry out textual criticism of the Greek text of the Old Testament. This is far from an easy task, but it is necessary before the Septuagint can be used to assist in the textual criticism of the Hebrew text.[64] Once an original Greek text is available, the text critic must deter-

---

60. Kenyon, *Our Bible and the Ancient Manuscripts*, 76–78.
61. *Old Testament in Greek* (Brooke–McLean), 1/1:vi.
62. Ibid., vii.
63. Klein, *Textual Criticism*, 51–53.
64. Kenyon, *Our Bible and the Ancient Manuscripts*, 92.

mine if the translator correctly rendered the Hebrew text (e.g., the Septuagint is notorious for incorrectly translating certain technical terms in the Psalms superscriptions). A factor that complicates this stage in the process is the variation from book to book in the quality of the translation in the Septuagint. Ralph Klein presents evidence that the quality of the translation can vary even within a book of the Greek Old Testament.[65] A difference in the Greek text may also be due to a different understanding of the vowel tradition of the Hebrew text. While there was some use of *matres lectionis* in the Hebrew text from which the Septuagint was translated, there was no full graphic representation of vowels at that time (third to second centuries B.C.).[66] A variant Greek text may also sometimes indicate only a different word division resulting from occasional crowding in the Hebrew *Vorlage*. And finally, a different Greek text may indicate only that the Greek translator was translating more freely rather than more literally in a given text.[67] The conclusion is not that the Greek Old Testament has no place in Old Testament textual criticism. Rather, it is that the Septuagint should not be used to suggest wholesale changes in the Old Testament text. As with the Samaritan Pentateuch and the Targums, the Septuagint will need to be examined on a case-by-case basis. On occasion it will hold the key for determining the original text of the Old Testament (see figure 3).[68]

---

65. Klein, *Textual Criticism*, 67–68; he also suggests that different individuals translated different parts of the book of Jeremiah. Emanuel Tov, *The Septuagint Translation of Jeremiah and Baruch*, Harvard Semitic Monographs 8 (Missoula, Mont.: Scholars Press, 1976), 4–5, argues that an original translation of Jeremiah that was only partly revised better explains the data than a two-translator theory.

66. Bruce K. Waltke, "The Textual Criticism of the Old Testament," in *The Expositor's Bible Commentary*, ed. Frank E. Gaebelein (Grand Rapids: Zondervan, 1979), 1:218, 221, suggests that the Septuagint translators had a less adequate understanding of the vowel tradition of the Hebrew text than what was typical within mainstream Judaism.

67. These principles are developed from the discussion in Kenyon, *Our Bible and the Ancient Manuscripts*, 79, 92.

68. Chapter 7 further discusses the use of the various versions in Old Testament textual criticism.

FIGURE 3   GREEK VERSIONS

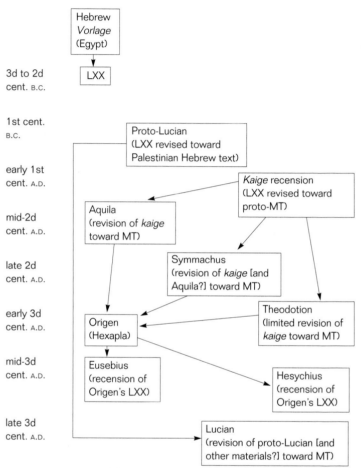

Source: Adapted from Kevin G. O'Connell, "Greek Versions (Minor)," in *The Interpreter's Dictionary of the Bible: Supplementary Volume*, ed. Keith Crim (Nashville: Abingdon, 1976), 377–81.

Other Important Ancient Versions

The versions already mentioned are the most important for the textual criticism of the Old Testament. However, for the sake of completeness, several others should be mentioned as this chapter is concluded. The first of these is the Peshitta, a

translation of the Old Testament in Syriac (a dialect of Aramaic).[69]
The Peshitta's origin and early history are not known. Some scholars hold that Aramaic Targums exercised an important influence on the Syriac translation, but others maintain that the translation was initially made from the Hebrew text.[70] Whatever the truth of its origin, the Peshitta was subsequently revised in the light of other texts and translations. Of these subsequent influences, the Septuagint had the largest impact on the Syriac renderings. The conclusion is thus that a Syriac agreement with the Septuagint against the Masoretic Text is not necessarily to be understood as the testimony of two separate witnesses. Such an agreement may only be the testimony of a single witness repeated two times.[71]

A second ancient version that is important for Old Testament textual criticism is the Old Latin or *Itala*. The Old Latin is a "daughter translation" (i.e., made from a translation—the Septuagint in this case—and not directly from the Hebrew text).[72] Actually, it might be more appropriate to speak of Old Latin translations, since the Old Latin exists in both an African and a European form.[73] This group of translations was

69. A modern critical edition of the Peshitta is being published by the Peshitta Institute of Leiden University. Publication began with a sample edition in 1966 containing the Song of Songs, Tobit, and 4 Ezra; a general preface was published in 1972: *The Old Testament in Syriac according to the Peshiṭta Version: General Preface*, ed. Pieter A. H. de Boer and Willem Baars (Leiden: Brill, 1972). Publication is not complete, but continues at present.

70. Würthwein, *Text of the Old Testament*, 80–81. Extensive work on the Peshitta of Exodus has been done by M. D. Koster, *The Peshiṭta of Exodus: The Development of Its Text in the Course of Fifteen Centuries*, Studia Semitica Neerlandica 19 (Amsterdam: van Gorcum, 1977). His conclusion (page 212), for the Book of Exodus, is that it is "a single translation of the Hebrew basic text into Syriac which in the course of time gradually moved further away from MT. . . . In as far as one can speak of a 'Targumisches Profil' in P[eshitta], this is therefore to be found not at the beginning but at the end of the development of its text."

71. Würthwein, *Text of the Old Testament*, 80–81.

72. Cross, "Theory of Local Texts," 312–13, suggests that the Old Latin may have been translated from the proto-Lucian recension.

73. Kenyon, *Our Bible and the Ancient Manuscripts*, 84. Würthwein, *Text of the Old Testament*, 88, adds that the European text is characterized by several different subgroups.

probably made sometime during the second century A.D., which means that it allows access to the Septuagint text prior to the time of the versions of Origen, Lucian, and Hesychius.[74] Thus its importance is greater for helping to determine the original text of the Greek Old Testament than of the Hebrew. In this fashion, however, the Old Latin allows for an indirect means of discussing the Hebrew text of the Old Testament.[75]

A final ancient version that is important for establishing the Old Testament text is the Latin Vulgate. By the middle of the fourth century A.D. the Old Latin was anything but uniform, and Jerome was therefore commissioned by Pope Damasus I in A.D. 382 to revise the Latin Bible (Old Latin). The work was carried out in stages. In an initial effort Jerome made minor revisions of the Book of Psalms on the basis of the Septuagint, which became known as the Roman Psalter. Somewhat later, Jerome made more extensive revisions to the Book of Psalms on the basis of both the Septuagint and the Hebrew text, making a version that became known as the Gallican Psalter. Finally, in a third stage, Jerome made a more complete revision of the entire Old Testament on the basis of the Hebrew text.[76] This last phase of Jerome's revision lasted from ca. A.D. 390 to 405.[77] At first Jerome's work met with a hostile reception, but by the beginning of the seventh century A.D. the Vulgate was accepted on an equal basis with the Old Latin. By the eighth and ninth centuries it superseded the Old Latin as the more accepted version, although both continued to be used in the church.[78] The Vulgate was adopted by the Roman Catholic Church as its official Bible at the Council of Trent in 1546. Two sanctioned editions were produced soon after. The first was a revision authorized by Pope Sixtus in

74. Kenyon, *Our Bible and the Ancient Manuscripts*, 84.

75. Würthwein, *Text of the Old Testament*, 87.

76. The Gallican Psalter replaced Jerome's version based on Hebrew in most manuscripts of the Vulgate after the time of Alcuin. Cf. *Biblia Sacra iuxta Vulgatam Versionem*, ed. Robert Weber et al., 3d ed. (Stuttgart: Deutsche Bibelgesellschaft, 1983), xxi. This edition of the Vulgate prints the Gallican Psalter and the Hebrew-based Psalter on opposite pages.

77. The situation for the New Testament is more complicated. Jerome revised the Gospels, but the revisers of the rest of the New Testament books are unknown (ibid., xx–xxi).

78. Würthwein, *Text of the Old Testament*, 93.

1589, the so-called Sixtine edition. A later, more careful edition was the Clementine, published by Pope Clement VIII in 1592 (see figure 4).[79]

FIGURE 4   LATIN VERSIONS

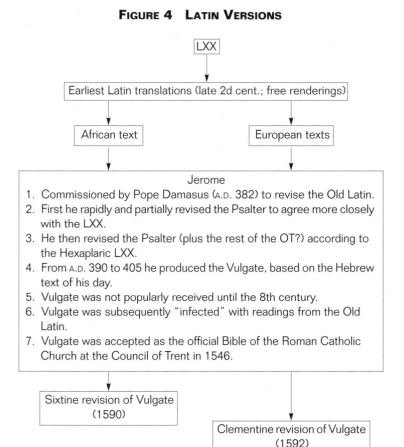

LXX

Earliest Latin translations (late 2d cent.; free renderings)

African text   European texts

Jerome
1. Commissioned by Pope Damasus (A.D. 382) to revise the Old Latin.
2. First he rapidly and partially revised the Psalter to agree more closely with the LXX.
3. He then revised the Psalter (plus the rest of the OT?) according to the Hexaplaric LXX.
4. From A.D. 390 to 405 he produced the Vulgate, based on the Hebrew text of his day.
5. Vulgate was not popularly received until the 8th century.
6. Vulgate was subsequently "infected" with readings from the Old Latin.
7. Vulgate was accepted as the official Bible of the Roman Catholic Church at the Council of Trent in 1546.

Sixtine revision of Vulgate
(1590)

Clementine revision of Vulgate
(1592)

Sources: Adapted from Ernst Würthwein, *The Text of the Old Testament,* trans. Erroll F. Rhodes (Grand Rapids: Eerdmans, 1979), 87–95; and Bleddyn J. Roberts, "The Old Testament: Manuscripts, Text and Versions," in *The Cambridge History of the Bible,* vol. 2: *The West from the Fathers to the Reformation,* ed. Geoffrey W. H. Lampe (Cambridge: Cambridge University Press, 1969), 24–25.

79. Ibid., 94.

FIGURE 5 HISTORY OF THE OLD TESTAMENT TEXT

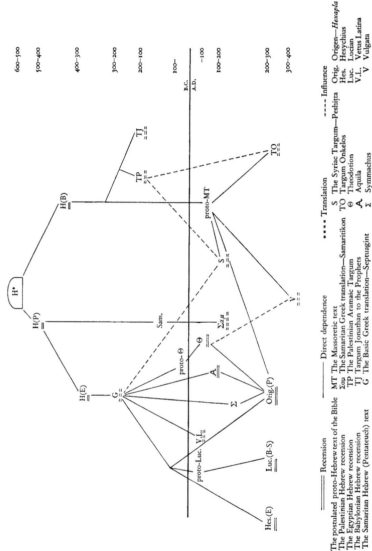

Source: Shemaryahu Talmon, "The Old Testament Text," in *The Cambridge History of the Bible,* vol. 1: *From the Beginnings to Jerome,* ed. R. Ackroyd and Christopher F. Evans (Cambridge: Cambridge University Press, 1970), 195. Reproduced with permission.

The Vulgate is important as a witness to the Hebrew text, but its importance is less than might appear to be the case at first glance. Though it was made with reference to the Hebrew text, its usefulness for textual criticism is affected by its variable character as a translation,[80] by its coexistence alongside the Old Latin throughout long periods, and by its interdependence on the Septuagint.[81]

The scope of this book precludes any detailed discussion of other ancient versions of the Old Testament. Information about these versions—Coptic, Ethiopic, Armenian, and Arabic—can be found in various sources.[82] These last mentioned versions are all "daughter" translations made from the Septuagint, and therefore they are only of indirect usefulness for establishing the text of the Hebrew Bible.[83]

Figure 5 contains in chart form an overview of the history of the Old Testament text.

80. Kenyon, *Our Bible and the Ancient Manuscripts*, 88, says that some parts are freely translated and others are very literal.

81. Würthwein, *Text of the Old Testament*, 93–94.

82. See, e.g., ibid., 96–100; and Roberts, *Old Testament Text*, 229–36, 266–69.

83. Kenyon, *Our Bible and the Ancient Manuscripts*, 89. This judgment is not completely true, since a part of the Arabic version of the Old Testament was produced by Saadia Gaon on the basis of the Hebrew. Only part of this work has survived, and other parts of the Arabic version of the Old Testament were made from the Septuagint, the Peshitta, and other versions. The reference to an Arabic Old Testament is thus a reference to a nonuniform textual tradition. Cf. Würthwein, *Text of the Old Testament*, 100.

4

The Dead Sea Scrolls

Having discussed the history of the transmission of the Old Testament text in both Hebrew and the ancient versions, it is appropriate to make some general comments on the justly famous Dead Sea Scrolls.[1] These ancient documents need to be treated in their own right so that their significance within the larger history of the Old Testament text will be clear. Many entire books have been devoted to the story of the discovery and the significance of the Dead Sea Scrolls.[2] Clearly that kind of detail will not be possible in this chapter, but the following pages will review important elements of the discovery, extent, and significance of these ancient documents.

Discovery

The account of the initial discovery of ancient manuscripts in 1947 in the vicinity of the Dead Sea has been told many times. Indeed, according to some writers, the exact details

1. Scholars dispute the utility of the term Dead Sea Scrolls. As some point out, the scrolls certainly were not discovered in the Dead Sea. Yet the name seems to have become the most used, even though other names such as Qumran Library or Essene Documents have been suggested from time to time.
2. For accounts of the discovery and significance of the Qumran documents, see Frank M. Cross Jr., *The Ancient Library of Qumran and Modern Biblical Studies*, rev. ed. (Garden City, N.Y.: Doubleday, 1961; reprinted Grand Rapids: Baker, 1980); and Millar Burrows, *The Dead Sea Scrolls* (New York: Viking, 1955).

are beyond recovery at present.[3] In general terms, however, in February or March 1947, two Bedouin shepherds accidentally discovered what later came to be known as Qumran cave 1.[4] In the cave they found several jars, most of which were broken, containing leather scrolls wrapped in linen. A total of eleven scrolls were found in this initial discovery. Five subsequently came into the possession of Archbishop Samuel of the Syrian Orthodox Monastery of St. Mark, while the others were eventually purchased by Professor Eleazar L. Sukenik of the Hebrew University of Jerusalem.[5]

The initial find of eleven scrolls represented seven different manuscripts of six different works. Most important were two different manuscripts of the Book of Isaiah. The first, called the *St. Mark's Isaiah Scroll* and later designated as 1QIsa[a], is a complete copy of the Book of Isaiah.[6] The great Isaiah scroll is about 24 feet long with a width between 9.5 and 10.5 inches. The 54 columns of text are included on 17 sheets of leather sewn together to form the scroll. A second copy of the Book of Isaiah, acquired by the Hebrew University, is an incomplete manuscript (1QIsa[b]). It is poorly preserved and contains portions of chapters 10, 13, 16, 19–30, and 35–66. A third biblical scroll found in cave 1 is a commentary (*pesher*) on Habakkuk 1–2 (1QpHab). It contains the biblical text interspersed with commentary that relates the prophecy to events contemporary with the date of the commentary's composition. A curiosity of the Habakkuk commentary is that

---

3. Burrows, *Dead Sea Scrolls*, 4. As André Dupont-Sommer, *The Essene Writings from Qumran*, trans. Geza Vermes (Cleveland: World, 1962), 2, mentions, even the date of the initial discovery is disputed. The Bedouin discoverers first reported that the manuscripts were initially found in 1947, but their later reports mentioned 1945. Most accept the originally mentioned date as authentic.

4. Burrows, *Dead Sea Scrolls*, 4.

5. Ibid., 5–6, 19.

6. Ibid., 19. The sigla used for the Dead Sea Scrolls indicate the cave where the manuscript was found (numbers 1–11) at Qumran (Q), the identity of the scroll, and the order of the find (or importance of the find) (superscript a, b, etc.). Other sigla preceding the name of the biblical book include the letter *p* (to indicate a *pesher*, or commentary, on that book), the abbreviation LXX (to indicate that the item is written in Greek), and the word *paleo* (to indicate that the scroll or fragment is written in the paleo-Hebrew script).

the divine name is written in the paleo-Hebrew script, while the rest of the text is written in the square script.[7] The other manuscripts found in Qumran cave 1 were all nonbiblical scrolls. The first, initially called *Manual of Discipline* by Millar Burrows, was found on two different scroll portions (separated prior to discovery).[8] This scroll, now designated as 1QS, preserves 11 columns of text on a scroll 6.5 feet long by 10 inches wide. There are reportedly many corrections and erasures that can be seen on the scroll.[9] An Aramaic scroll was also found in cave 1, but its condition did not allow it to be unrolled until later. It was called the *Lamech Scroll* by Burrows but subsequently it became known as the *Genesis Apocryphon*.[10] A third work discovered in cave 1 is known as the *War Scroll* (1QM). It describes a pitched battle between the "Sons of Light" and the "Sons of Darkness." The final major work found in the initial discovery was represented on four fragments and is known as the *Thanksgiving Psalms*.

Some of the individuals to whom the scrolls were first offered for sale did not recognize their worth.[11] Even after William F. Albright and others dated these early finds to the last centuries B.C., other scholars maintained a skeptical attitude. Some questioned the early date because archeologists never saw the scrolls *in situ*, especially in the jars in which they had supposedly been discovered. Roland de Vaux was finally able to lay this skepticism to rest when he published his archeological findings from several seasons of excavation at Khirbet Qumran and the various caves nearby. His summary regarding the discovery of the scrolls affirms that the scrolls were found in the caves, that the manuscripts were ancient, and that the documents were deposited in the caves in ancient times.[12] The evidence that sustains these conclusions includes trained ex-

---

7. William S. LaSor, *The Dead Sea Scrolls and the New Testament* (Grand Rapids: Eerdmans, 1972), 29–30.

8. Burrows, *Dead Sea Scrolls*, 19.

9. LaSor, *Dead Sea Scrolls*, 30.

10. Burrows, *Dead Sea Scrolls*, 19; LaSor, *Dead Sea Scrolls*, 31.

11. Burrows, *Dead Sea Scrolls*, 7.

12. Roland de Vaux, *Archaeology and the Dead Sea Scrolls*, rev. ed., Schweich Lectures 1959 (London: Oxford University Press for the British Academy, 1973), 95.

cavators finding further fragments in cave 1 that were either similar to or actually part of earlier manuscript finds. The antiquity of the manuscripts is supported by several independent lines of evidence. The paleographic study of the manuscripts, the dating of the pottery and the coins discovered at Qumran and in the caves, and carbon-14 analysis of samples of the linen coverings of the manuscripts all coincide in establishing a general date of the last two centuries B.C. and the first century A.D. for the scrolls and their placement in the caves near Qumran.[13] That several text types (see further in this chapter) existed side by side at Qumran helps to date the manuscripts.

Since cave 1 was excavated in 1949, more than two hundred caves have been examined in the region near Qumran. Of these, twenty-five were found to contain pottery of the same type as cave 1, and eleven caves contained manuscript fragments that were similar to the "original" Dead Sea Scrolls. A survey of the contents of these eleven manuscript-bearing caves is the subject of the next section.

Contents

Though the biblical scrolls are most crucial to the aims of this book, it is important to set them in the overall context of the "Qumran Library holdings." In addition to the biblical manuscripts, several deuterocanonical or apocryphal works were represented at Qumran. These include examples of Tobit, Ecclesiasticus (or the Wisdom of Ben Sirach), and the Epistle of Jeremy. Tobit is represented by three manuscripts in Aramaic and one in Hebrew. Jozef T. Milik considers that the work may have been written originally in Aramaic.[14] A few fragments of the Hebrew original of Ecclesiasticus (6:20–31) were found in cave 2, while some papyrus fragments in cave 7 seem to give part of the Epistle of Jeremy in Greek.[15]

13. Ibid., 97–101. The carbon-14 date for the linen fragments was A.D. 33 ± 200 years.
14. Jozef T. Milik, *Ten Years of Discovery in the Wilderness of Judaea*, trans. John Strugnell, Studies in Biblical Theology 26 (London: SCM, 1959), 31.
15. Ibid., 32.

Caves 1, 2, and 4 have yielded parts of about ten manuscripts of the pseudepigraphical work known as Jubilees. Another pseudepigraphical work found at Qumran is the Book of Enoch, represented by ten fragments from cave 4. An Aramaic *Testament of Levi*, found in fragmentary form in caves 1 and 4, may represent part of the sources used in composing the *Testaments of the Twelve Patriarchs*.[16]

A major part of the Qumran finds has been classed as sectarian literature. This category refers to literature composed by the members of the presumably Essene community that lived in and around Qumran during parts of the last two centuries B.C. and the first century A.D. The most important of these works is now known as the *Rule of the Community* (1QS; originally called the *Manual of Discipline*). This composition is known from an almost complete manuscript from cave 1 and ten fragmentary copies from cave 4. The work includes, among other things, liturgies, doctrine, and regulations for the community life.[17] A second important sectarian document is known as the *Damascus Document*, which "comments on God's saving plan in history . . . [and] gives detailed rules for the lives of members of the New Covenant in their camps in the land of Damascus."[18] It was previously known from two manuscripts found in the Cairo Geniza at the turn of the century. Copies were found in caves 4, 5, and 6.[19]

Also classed as sectarian works are the *Rule for the Final War* and various copies of sectarian hymns. A long scroll called *Hodayot* (hymns) was found in cave 1, a poorly preserved copy of sectarian hymns (1QH). Six fragmentary copies of these hymns were also found in cave 4.[20] The copy found in cave 1 contains about twenty psalms. They echo the language of the biblical psalms, but do not have the same prophetic force or originality as the Old Testament Psalter.[21]

---

16. Ibid., 32–37. Milik lists other documentary remains that are also to be classed as Old Testament Pseudepigrapha.
17. Ibid., 37.
18. Ibid., 38.
19. Ibid.
20. Ibid., 39–40.
21. Burrows, *Dead Sea Scrolls*, 27–28.

A final type of sectarian work includes the commentaries (*pesharim*) on various biblical books. In a sense, these represent a mixed category. They include biblical text, but the portions of an Old Testament book are interspersed with commentary supplied by members of the community. Commentaries have been discovered for Habakkuk, Micah, Psalms, Nahum, and Isaiah. The first three reflect a kind of exegesis where the Old Testament text is explained in connection to the community's own history. The *pesher* of Nahum explains the text in relation to events that were contemporary with the days of the community's existence at Qumran. The commentary of Isaiah reflects a more traditional type of exegesis, that is, seeking to give the meaning intended by the sacred author.[22] These commentaries are somewhat similar to the Qumran works known as *Testimonia* and *florilegium*, although these latter contain commentary on a selected group of isolated verses rather than connected sections of Old Testament text.[23]

The eleven caves have provided the scholarly world with fragments of about six hundred books. Of these, approximately one-quarter are biblical manuscripts. There are at least fragments of all the Old Testament books except for the Book of Esther.[24] A survey of the representation of Old Testament books at Qumran can be seen in table 8.

The great majority of the Qumran biblical scrolls are written in the square script, and a minority are written in the paleo-Hebrew script. According to Judith Sanderson, there are sixteen paleo-Hebrew scrolls known from the Qumran caves: twelve of the Torah, one of Job, one nonbiblical scroll, and two still unidentified.[25]

The Qumran biblical scrolls written in Hebrew do not present a uniform text type, but reflect different types of text. Earlier studies spoke of the existence of three text types at Qumran, but more recent studies refer to five groups of

22. Milik, *Ten Years of Discovery*, 40.
23. Ibid., 41. Milik also lists some additional miscellaneous documents on pages 41–42.
24. Dupont-Sommer, *Essene Writings*, 3.
25. Judith E. Sanderson, "The Contributions of 4QPaleoExod^m to Textual Criticism," *Revue de Qumran* 13 (1988): 547.

TABLE 8   BIBLICAL TEXTS
FROM QUMRAN (BY CAVE NO.)

	#1	#4	#11	other
Genesis	1	12		3
Exodus	1	12		3
Leviticus	1	4	1	2
Numbers	1	2		3
Deuteronomy	2	18		5
Joshua		2		
Judges	1	2		
Samuel	1	3		
Kings		1		2
Isaiah	2	15		1
Jeremiah		3		1
Ezekiel	1	1	1	1
The Twelve		7		1
Psalms	3	17	3	4
Job		3		1
Proverbs		2		
Ruth		2		2
Song of Songs		3		1
Ecclesiastes		2		
Lamentations		1		3
Daniel	2	5		1
Ezra–Nehemiah		1		
Chronicles		1		

Source: Patrick W. Skehan, "The Biblical Scrolls from Qumran and the Text of
the Old Testament," in *Qumran and the History of the Biblical Text,* ed. Frank
M. Cross and Shemaryahu Talmon (Cambridge: Harvard University Press,
1975), 265. The last column groups together caves 2, 3, and 5–10, the so-
called minor caves.

texts.[26] First, there are biblical scrolls that essentially reflect the text that later came to be known as the Masoretic Text; these are called proto-Masoretic. It is estimated that 60% of the Qumran biblical scrolls fall under this classification.[27] A second group of Qumran texts is very close to what later became known as the Samaritan Pentateuch. Once called proto-Samaritan, these should be more correctly referred to as pre-Samaritan.[28] A third grouping of Qumran manuscripts reflects a text that is close to the *Vorlage* of the Septuagint. The pre-Samaritan and Septuagint-type manuscripts at Qumran together account for about 5% of the biblical manuscripts. There are additional manuscripts among the Dead Sea biblical scrolls that are either nonaligned (i.e., of mixed text type) or that reflect "Qumran practice," that is, scribal practices and characteristic spellings known from scrolls found at Qumran. In the opinion of Emanuel Tov, only this last group of scrolls was actually produced in Qumran.[29]

Significance

Frank M. Cross has indicated something of the areas touched by the discovery of these ancient documents, both biblical and nonbiblical. The Qumran documents have influenced the following areas of Old Testament study: canon, the development of Hebrew and Aramaic dialects, ancient scripts, orthographies, scribal practices, historical criticism, and textual criticism.[30] It is this latter significance that is most important to the topic of this book.

The significance of the Qumran documents to textual criticism can be summarized in three propositions. First and foremost, the Dead Sea Scrolls take the textual scholar back

26. Emanuel Tov, *Textual Criticism of the Hebrew Bible* (Minneapolis: Fortress, 1992), 114–17.
27. Ibid., 115. See also Bruce K. Waltke, "Old Testament Textual Criticism," in *Holman Introduction to the Bible*, ed. David S. Dockery, Kenneth A. Mathews, and Robert Sloan (Nashville: Broadman, forthcoming).
28. Tov, *Textual Criticism of the Hebrew Bible*, 19, 81–82.
29. Ibid., 116–17.
30. Cross, *Ancient Library of Qumran*, 163.

around one thousand years earlier than previously known Hebrew manuscript evidence. Prior to the Qumran discoveries, the earliest complete copies of Old Testament books dated from about the early tenth century A.D. The earliest complete copy of the entire Old Testament dated from the early eleventh century A.D.[31] The Dead Sea manuscripts thus give much earlier evidence for the text of the Old Testament than anything that was previously known.

A related issue concerns the overall relationship between the relatively late Masoretic manuscripts and the texts discovered at Qumran. While there are many small differences between the Masoretic Text and the various Qumran documents, the overall agreement between them is striking. Burrows wrote the following in regard to the complete Isaiah scroll:

> The conspicuous differences in spelling and grammatical forms between the St. Mark's manuscript and the Masoretic text makes their substantial agreement in the words of the text all the more remarkable. . . . It is a matter for wonder that through something like a thousand years the text underwent so little alteration. As I said in my first article on the scroll, "Herein lies its chief importance, supporting the fidelity of the Masoretic tradition."[32]

Thus the Qumran scrolls, while being much earlier than the Masoretic Text, generally support the fidelity with which the Masoretic Text was copied.

The third statement concerning the significance of the Dead Sea Scrolls has to do with the details of the preservation of the Old Testament text. While the Qumran documents have certified the overall faithfulness with which the text was copied, they also point out that the text in the last two centuries B.C., and up through at least a part of the first century A.D., existed in various text types rather than only one. Before the finds in the Judean desert, text critics could only work with the state of the text indirectly, that is, by suggesting an alternate form of the Hebrew text that was used by the translators

---

31. For details, see the development in chapter 2.
32. Burrows, *Dead Sea Scrolls*, 304.

of the Septuagint. The finds at Qumran have provided actual manuscripts with which the text critic can work. The great majority support the Masoretic Text, but there are also manuscripts that support the readings of the Septuagint and Samaritan Pentateuch, as well as others that are not aligned with any previously known text type. It is fair to say that the Qumran finds have revolutionized the field of textual criticism.[33]

33. The Dead Sea Scrolls are available in the official, ongoing series entitled *Discoveries in the Judaean Desert of Jordan* (Oxford: Clarendon, 1955–).

5

Introduction to *BHS*

This chapter aims to familiarize the reader with the overall format of *Biblia Hebraica Stuttgartensia* (*BHS*). The topics covered include page format, Masoretic notations, and textual apparatus.

Page Format

The following discussion uses the two sample pages of *BHS* that are included as figures 6–7. Figure 6 shows page 234 of *BHS*, which contains the text of Numbers 12:4–13:3; figure 7 shows page 141 of *BHS*, containing Exodus 32:16–30. Note that even-numbered pages are headed by the name of the book in unpointed Hebrew letters (see box A in figure 6); odd-numbered pages are headed by the name of the Old Testament book in Latin (box A in figure 7). On the opening page of all Old Testament books, whether odd or even, the name appears in both Hebrew and Latin.

There is an unpointed ס in line 1 of figure 6 (box B), which indicates a closed paragraph (i.e., started after a short space in the same line). There is also an unpointed פ in line 15 and again in line 19 (boxes C); these two letters indicate the start of an open paragraph (i.e., started on a new line in ancient manuscripts).

The large box D in the right margin of figure 6 encloses the Masorah parva (small Masorah). Immediately below the bib-

FIGURE 6 SAMPLE PAGE FROM *BHS*

234   **A** במדבר   12,4—13,3

D

4 הָֽאָדָם֙ אֲשֶׁ֣ר עַל־פְּנֵ֣י הָֽאֲדָמָֽה׃ ס **B** 4 וַיֹּ֨אמֶר יְהוָ֜ה פִּתְאֹ֗ם אֶל־
מֹשֶׁ֤ה וְאֶֽל־אַהֲרֹן֙ וְאֶל־מִרְיָ֔ם צְא֥וּ שְׁלָשְׁתְּכֶ֖ם אֶל־אֹ֣הֶל מוֹעֵ֑ד וַיֵּצְא֖וּ
5 שְׁלָשְׁתָּֽם׃ 5 וַיֵּ֤רֶד יְהוָה֙ בְּעַמּ֣וּד עָנָ֔ן וַֽיַּעֲמֹ֖ד פֶּ֣תַח הָאֹ֑הֶל וַיִּקְרָא֙ אַהֲרֹ֣ן
וּמִרְיָ֔ם וַיֵּצְא֖וּ שְׁנֵיהֶֽם׃ 6 וַיֹּ֖אמֶר
שִׁמְעוּ־נָ֣א דְבָרָ֑י אִם־יִֽהְיֶה֙ נְבִ֣יאֲכֶ֔ם יְהוָ֗ה
בַּמַּרְאָה֙ אֵלָ֣יו אֶתְוַדָּ֔ע בַּחֲל֖וֹם אֲדַבֶּר־בּֽוֹ׃
7 לֹא־כֵ֖ן עַבְדִּ֣י מֹשֶׁ֑ה בְּכָל־בֵּיתִ֖י נֶאֱמָ֥ן הֽוּא׃
8 פֶּ֣ה אֶל־פֶּ֞ה אֲדַבֶּר־בּ֗וֹ וּמַרְאֶה֙ וְלֹ֣א בְחִידֹ֔ת וּתְמֻנַ֥ת יְהוָ֖ה יַבִּ֑יט
וּמַדּ֙וּעַ֙ לֹ֣א יְרֵאתֶ֔ם לְדַבֵּ֖ר בְּעַבְדִּ֥י בְמֹשֶֽׁה׃
9/10 וַיִּֽחַר־אַ֧ף יְהוָ֛ה בָּ֖ם וַיֵּלַֽךְ׃ 10 וְהֶעָנָ֗ן סָ֚ר מֵעַ֣ל הָאֹ֔הֶל וְהִנֵּ֥ה מִרְיָ֖ם
מְצֹרַ֣עַת כַּשָּׁ֑לֶג וַיִּ֧פֶן אַהֲרֹ֛ן אֶל־מִרְיָ֖ם וְהִנֵּ֥ה מְצֹרָֽעַת׃ 11 וַיֹּ֥אמֶר
אַהֲרֹ֖ן אֶל־מֹשֶׁ֑ה בִּ֣י אֲדֹנִ֔י אַל־נָ֨א תָשֵׁ֤ת עָלֵ֙ינוּ֙ חַטָּ֔את אֲשֶׁ֥ר נוֹאַ֖לְנוּ
וַאֲשֶׁ֥ר חָטָֽאנוּ׃ 12 אַל־נָ֥א תְהִ֖י כַּמֵּ֑ת אֲשֶׁ֤ר בְּצֵאתוֹ֙ מֵרֶ֣חֶם אִמּ֔וֹ 12
13 וַיֵּעַ֣ל חֲצִ֣י בְשָׂרֽוֹ׃ 13 וַיִּצְעַ֣ק מֹשֶׁ֔ה אֶל־יְהוָ֖ה לֵאמֹ֑ר אֵ֕ל נָ֛א רְפָ֥א
נָ֖א לָֽהּ׃ ף **C** 14 וַיֹּ֨אמֶר יְהוָ֜ה אֶל־מֹשֶׁ֗ה וְאָבִ֙יהָ֙ יָרֹ֤ק יָרַק֙ בְּפָנֶ֔יהָ
הֲלֹ֥א תִכָּלֵ֖ם שִׁבְעַ֣ת יָמִ֑ים תִּסָּגֵ֞ר שִׁבְעַ֤ת יָמִים֙ מִח֣וּץ לַֽמַּחֲנֶ֔ה וְאַחַ֖ר
15 תֵּאָסֵֽף׃ 15 וַתִּסָּגֵ֥ר מִרְיָ֛ם מִח֥וּץ לַֽמַּחֲנֶ֖ה שִׁבְעַ֣ת יָמִ֑ים וְהָעָם֙ לֹ֣א נָסַ֔ע
16 עַד־הֵאָסֵ֖ף מִרְיָֽם׃ 16 וְאַחַ֛ר נָסְע֥וּ הָעָ֖ם מֵחֲצֵר֑וֹת וַֽיַּחֲנ֖וּ בְּמִדְבַּ֥ר
פָּארָֽן׃ ף **C**

G

13 1 וַיְדַבֵּ֥ר יְהוָ֖ה אֶל־מֹשֶׁ֥ה לֵּאמֹֽר׃ 2 שְׁלַח־לְךָ֣ אֲנָשִׁ֗ים וְיָתֻ֙רוּ֙
אֶת־אֶ֣רֶץ כְּנַ֔עַן אֲשֶׁר־אֲנִ֥י נֹתֵ֖ן לִבְנֵ֣י יִשְׂרָאֵ֑ל אִ֣ישׁ אֶחָד֩ אִ֨ישׁ אֶחָ֜ד
לְמַטֵּ֤ה אֲבֹתָיו֙ תִּשְׁלָ֔חוּ כֹּ֖ל נָשִׂ֥יא בָהֶֽם׃ 3 וַיִּשְׁלַ֨ח אֹתָ֥ם מֹשֶׁ֛ה מִמִּדְבַּ֥ר 3

E

Cp 12 ¹Mm 904. ²Mm 436. ³Mm 3925. ⁴Mm 539. ⁵Mm 1454. ⁶Mm 175. ⁷Mm 328. ⁸Mm 3298.
⁹Mm 751.

F

4 ᵃ⁻ᵃ 𝔊* invers cf 1 ‖ 5 ᵃ ᴍˢˢ העʹ ‖ ᵇ 1 וַיָּבֹ֙אוּ? cf 11,24ᵃ ‖ 6 ᵃ tr huc יהוה ex 6b;
𝔊(𝔖) + 𝔊ᴸ[𝔖] κύριος) πρὸς αὐτούς ‖ ᶜ 1 נְבִיאֲ בָכֶם cf 𝔙 ‖ ᶜ dl, cf ᵃ; 𝔊(𝔙) κυρίῳ =
ליהוה; 𝔖(ℭ) ʼnʼ mrjʼ = אֲנִי יהוה ‖ ᵈ ᴍ התʹ ‖ ᵉ 1 c 𝔊𝔖𝔙 בְּמֹ ᴍ ‖ 8 ᵃ pc Mss 𝔊𝔖ℭ
‖ 𝔖(ℭ) ʼnʼ mrjʼ =, prp וְאָמְרָה, dl (gl ad ותמנת cf ᵇ) ‖ ᵇ 𝔊(𝔖) καὶ τὴν δόξαν cf ℭ ‖ 9 ᵃ⁻ᵃ sic L, mlt
Mss Edd וַיָּחַר־אַף ‖ 11 ᵃ ᴍ תשית ‖ 12 ᵃ ᴍ תהיה; 𝔖 nhwʼ = יְהִי ‖ ᵇ 𝔊(𝔙) + ὡσεὶ
ἔκτρωμα ‖ ᶜ Tiq soph pro אִמֵּנוּ et בְּשָׂרֵנוּ; 𝔊(𝔙) τῶν σαρκῶν αὐτῆς ‖ 13 ᵃ 1 אֵ֔ל ‖ 14 ᵃ
nonn vb exc? ‖ 15 ᵃ ᴍ נסעו ‖ ᵇ ᴍ פֶּה— 𝔊 ἐκαθαρίσθη ‖ 16 ᵃ 𝔅 hic incip cp 13 (cf
𝔊𝔙) ‖ ᵇ ut 10,12ᵃ ‖ Cp 13,1 ᵃ ᴍ𝔊ᵐⁱⁿ Syh pr vb sec Dt 1,20—23a ‖ 2 ᵃ ᴍ𝔊𝔖 sg.

FIGURE 7 SAMPLE PAGE FROM *BHS*

32,16—30 **A** EXODUS 141

16 מִשְּׁנֵי עֶבְרֵיהֶם מִזֶּה וּמִזֶּה הֵם כְּתֻבִים׃ וְהַ֨לֻּחֹ֔ת מַעֲשֵׂ֤ה אֱלֹהִים֙

17 הֵ֔מָּה וְהַמִּכְתָּ֗ב מִכְתַּ֤ב אֱלֹהִים֙ ה֔וּא חָר֖וּת עַל־הַלֻּחֹֽת׃ וַיִּשְׁמַ֧ע

יְהוֹשֻׁ֛עַ אֶת־ק֥וֹל הָעָ֖ם בְּרֵעֹ֑ה וַיֹּ֨אמֶר֙ אֶל־מֹשֶׁ֔ה ק֥וֹל מִלְחָמָ֖ה בַּֽמַּחֲנֶֽה׃

18 וַיֹּ֗אמֶר אֵ֥ין קוֹל֙ עֲנ֣וֹת גְּבוּרָ֔ה

וְאֵ֥ין ק֖וֹל עֲנ֣וֹת חֲלוּשָׁ֑ה

ק֣וֹל עַנּ֔וֹת אָנֹכִ֖י שֹׁמֵֽעַ׃

19 וַֽיְהִ֗י כַּאֲשֶׁ֤ר קָרַב֙ אֶל־הַֽמַּחֲנֶ֔ה וַיַּ֥רְא אֶת־הָעֵ֖גֶל וּמְחֹלֹ֑ת וַיִּֽחַר־

20 אַ֣ף מֹשֶׁ֗ה וַיַּשְׁלֵ֤ךְ מִיָּדָו֙ אֶת־הַלֻּחֹ֔ת וַיְשַׁבֵּ֥ר אֹתָ֖ם תַּ֣חַת הָהָֽר׃ וַיִּקַּ֞ח

אֶת־הָעֵ֨גֶל אֲשֶׁ֤ר עָשׂוּ֙ וַיִּשְׂרֹ֣ף בָּאֵ֔שׁ וַיִּטְחַ֖ן עַ֣ד אֲשֶׁר־דָּ֑ק וַיִּ֙זֶר֙ עַל־פְּנֵ֣י

21 הַמַּ֔יִם וַיַּ֖שְׁקְ אֶת־בְּנֵ֥י יִשְׂרָאֵֽל׃ וַיֹּ֤אמֶר מֹשֶׁה֙ אֶֽל־אַהֲרֹ֔ן מֶֽה־עָשָׂ֥ה

22 לְךָ֖ הָעָ֣ם הַזֶּ֑ה כִּֽי־הֵבֵ֥אתָ עָלָ֖יו חֲטָאָ֥ה גְדֹלָֽה׃ וַיֹּ֣אמֶר אַהֲרֹ֔ן אַל־

23 יִ֥חַר אַ֣ף אֲדֹנִ֑י אַתָּה֙ יָדַ֣עְתָּ אֶת־הָעָ֔ם כִּ֥י בְרָ֖ע הֽוּא׃ וַיֹּ֣אמְרוּ לִ֔י

עֲשֵׂה־לָ֣נוּ אֱלֹהִ֗ים אֲשֶׁ֤ר יֵֽלְכוּ֙ לְפָנֵ֔ינוּ כִּי־זֶ֣ה ׀ מֹשֶׁ֣ה הָאִ֗ישׁ אֲשֶׁ֤ר הֶֽעֱלָ֙נוּ֙

24 מֵאֶ֣רֶץ מִצְרַ֔יִם לֹ֥א יָדַ֖עְנוּ מֶה־הָ֥יָה לֽוֹ׃ וָאֹמַ֤ר לָהֶם֙ לְמִ֣י זָהָ֔ב

25 הִתְפָּרָ֔קוּ וַיִּתְּנוּ־לִ֑י וָאַשְׁלִכֵ֣הוּ בָאֵ֔שׁ וַיֵּצֵ֖א הָעֵ֥גֶל הַזֶּֽה׃ וַיַּ֤רְא מֹשֶׁה֙

26 אֶת־הָעָ֔ם כִּ֥י פָרֻ֖עַ ה֑וּא כִּֽי־פְרָעֹ֣ה אַהֲרֹ֔ן לְשִׁמְצָ֖ה בְּקָמֵיהֶֽם׃ וַיַּעֲמֹ֤ד

מֹשֶׁה֙ בְּשַׁ֣עַר הַֽמַּחֲנֶ֔ה וַיֹּ֕אמֶר מִ֥י לַיהוָ֖ה אֵלָ֑י וַיֵּאָסְפ֥וּ אֵלָ֖יו כָּל־בְּנֵ֥י

27 לֵוִֽי׃ וַיֹּ֣אמֶר לָהֶ֗ם כֹּֽה־אָמַ֤ר יְהוָה֙ אֱלֹהֵ֣י יִשְׂרָאֵ֔ל שִׂ֥ימוּ אִישׁ־חַרְבּ֖וֹ

עַל־יְרֵכ֑וֹ עִבְר֨וּ וָשׁ֜וּבוּ מִשַּׁ֤עַר לָשַׁ֙עַר֙ בַּֽמַּחֲנֶ֔ה וְהִרְג֧וּ אִֽישׁ־אֶת־אָחִ֛יו

28 וְאִ֥ישׁ אֶת־רֵעֵ֖הוּ וְאִ֥ישׁ אֶת־קְרֹבֽוֹ׃ וַיַּֽעֲשׂ֥וּ בְנֵֽי־לֵוִ֖י כִּדְבַ֣ר מֹשֶׁ֑ה

29 וַיִּפֹּ֤ל מִן־הָעָם֙ בַּיּ֣וֹם הַה֔וּא כִּשְׁלֹ֥שֶׁת אַלְפֵ֖י אִֽישׁ׃ וַיֹּ֣אמֶר מֹשֶׁ֗ה

מִלְא֨וּ יֶדְכֶ֤ם הַיּוֹם֙ לַֽיהוָ֔ה כִּ֛י אִ֥ישׁ בִּבְנ֖וֹ וּבְאָחִ֑יו וְלָתֵ֧ת עֲלֵיכֶ֛ם

30 הַיּ֖וֹם בְּרָכָֽה׃ וַֽיְהִי֙ מִֽמָּחֳרָ֔ת וַיֹּ֤אמֶר מֹשֶׁה֙ אֶל־הָעָ֔ם אַתֶּ֥ם

חֲטָאתֶ֖ם חֲטָאָ֣ה גְדֹלָ֑ה וְעַתָּה֙ אֶֽעֱלֶ֣ה אֶל־יְהוָ֔ה אוּלַ֥י אֲכַפְּרָ֖ה בְּעַ֥ד

20 Mm 598, Q^occ addidi, Or sine Q, cf Mp sub loco. 21 Mm 1269. 22 Mm 2421. 23 Mm 592. 24 Mm 599.
25 Mm 598. 26 Mm 11. 27 Mm 1087. 28 Mm 600. 29 Mm 601. 30 Gn 32,21.

17 ᵃ sic L, mlt Mss Edd —גָה || 18 ᵃ 𝔊^Fᵉᵐⁱⁿ(𝔉𝔖) + Μωυσῆς || ᵇ 𝔊 + οἴνου cf 𝔏, frt exc vb || 19 ᵃ ᵐˢˢ𝔊 || 22 ᵃ⁻ᵃ 𝔊 τὸ ὅρμημα (= עֶבְרַת =? בְּתַחְתִּית 𝔖𝔗𝔙) || ᵇ וְאֶת־הָם ᵐˢˢ𝔗𝔙 || τοῦ λαοῦ τούτου || ᵇ ᵐˢ פָּרוּעַ cf 25 || 27 ᵃ⁻ᵃ𝔊𝔖 וְעַ' || 29 ᵃ 𝔊(𝔙) ἐπληρώσατε || ᵇ nonn Mss ᵐˢ𝔊𝔖𝔗𝔙 יֶדְכֶם || ᶜ > 𝔊𝔖𝔙 || ᵈ 𝔊𝔖𝔙 om cop || 30 ᵃ 𝔊 τὸν θεόν || ᵇ ᵐˢ הַר.

lical text is box E, which encloses the register of the Masorah magna (large Masorah). Note that this register begins with the letters Cp 12, which indicates that the following Masorah magna entries deal with chapter 12 of the text. Note that the Masorah magna register is accessed by very small superscript numbers from entries in the Masorah parva. The entries Mm 904, etc., refer to particular lists in the separately published volume of the Masorah magna.[1]

Immediately below this Masorah magna register is box F, which encloses the apparatus that lists textual variants. A detailed introduction to the use of the textual apparatus will be given in the last section of this chapter.

Finally, for the sake of completeness, note box G in the left margin. These symbols refer to the liturgical divisions of the text. The large ס with a special mark above it indicates the start of a Seder, one of the 167 divisions of the Torah that were used in Palestinian circles for the public reading of the Torah in worship.[2] Note that this large ס is followed by two small Hebrew consonants within brackets and that each of these consonants has a small dot over it. These dotted Hebrew consonants indicate the number of the Seder for the particular book (in this case, Numbers). The numbering of the Sedarim begins with 1 for each successive book. פרש, the three consonants immediately below the ס, indicate that a Parashah also begins at this same point in the text. Babylonian Jews divided the Torah into 54 Parashoth, and by reading one a week it was possible to finish the Torah in a year.[3] Since there are about three times as many Sedarim as Parashoth, about every third Seder coincides with a new Parashah. On occasion, however, the (third) Seder and the Parashah do not begin at the same point.[4]

---

1. Gérard E. Weil, *Massorah Gedolah iuxta Codicem Leningradensem B19a*, vol. 1: *Catalogi* (Rome: Pontifical Biblical Institute Press, 1971).

2. Ernst Würthwein, *The Text of the Old Testament*, trans. Erroll F. Rhodes (Grand Rapids: Eerdmans, 1979), 21, mentions 452 Sedarim, but this number includes readings from the Early and Latter Prophets as well.

3. Ibid.

4. See, e.g., Exodus 30. A new Seder begins at 30:1, but the corresponding Parashah begins at 30:11.

Masoretic Notations

The beginning or intermediate Hebrew student will find the Masorah parva difficult to use, mainly because it is written in unpointed Hebrew or Aramaic and the style of writing is terse and abounds with abbreviations.[5] There are, however, two types of information given in the Masorah parva that are important for the intermediate Hebrew student: Kethiv-Qere and *hapax legomenon*.

First, then, is the indication of a Kethiv-Qere. In figure 7 the Masorah parva is enclosed in box B (the Masorah parva is always in the outer margin of *BHS*—on the left in figure 7 and on the right in figure 6). Box C further encloses a note indicating a Qere. The lower half of the two-tiered reading on the right side consists of the letter ק with a dot over it. This abbreviation for קְרֵא (Qere, "what is read") is keyed to the text by a small circle placed above the word מְיָדוֹ[6] and signals that the consonantal spelling of the Kethiv found in the text is to be read as indicated by the Hebrew word written in the Masorah parva with only consonants: מידיו.[7] The Kethiv and the Qere in this example differ only in consonantal spelling. The Kethiv, מידו, could be read either מִיָּדוֹ (singular) or מִיָּדוֹ (defectively written plural). The Qere reflects the normal (*plene*) spelling of the plural form. The rest of the note in the Masorah parva (חד מן ה̇ כת̇ חס̇) reads "one [time] out of five [occasions where this word is] written defec-

5. Two convenient works that introduce the student to the Masorah are Reinhard Wonneberger, *Understanding BHS: A Manual for the Users of Biblia Hebraica Stuttgartensia*, trans. Dwight R. Daniels, 2d ed. (Rome: Pontifical Biblical Institute Press, 1990), and William R. Scott, *A Simplified Guide to BHS* (Berkeley: BIBAL, 1987).

6. When a note refers to two or more words, placement of the circle is more complicated. See *BHS*, xvii–xviii. The beginning Hebrew student should be careful not to confuse the small circles that indicate Masorah parva notes with the circular parts of certain Masoretic accents; cf. the list of accents printed on a small card that accompanies *BHS*.

7. It is important to remember that the full spelling in the text represents a hybrid form—the consonants of the text represent the Kethiv, but the vowels represent the Qere—that is actually an "impossible" form. Such a hybrid spelling is behind the divine name Anglicized as *Jehovah*, made up of the consonants יהוה (*yhwh*) and vowels from אֲדֹנָי (Adonai).

tively."[8] The entire Masoretic notation indicates that this case of Kethiv-Qere only deals with a spelling variant. Without the qualifying note, the text critic would have had to determine if the Kethiv reflected a textual variant מִיָּדוֹ ("from his hand") or simply the spelling variant of the defectively written plural.

The Masorah parva also indicates when a word is used only once or spelled a certain way only once in the Old Testament. The note for a *hapax legomenon* in the Masorah parva is the letter ל with a small dot over it. A check of figure 7, verse 24, shows two words with circles over them, and in each case the note in the Masorah parva shows a dotted ל. This means that both words as written in this verse are unique in the Old Testament. A check of Mandelkern's concordance shows that הִתְפָּרְקוּ and וָאֶשְׁלְכֵהוּ are used only once in the Old Testament in these particular conjugated forms or particular spellings.[9] In these two cases the information gained is perhaps not highly significant, but in other cases this easily accessible information about words appearing only once in the entire Old Testament may prove very useful.

Textual Apparatus

At the bottom of the *BHS* page is the textual apparatus, listing selected readings that do not appear in Codex Leningradensis, the text on which the *BHS* edition is based. When a single word in the text is discussed in the textual apparatus, the word is followed in the text by a raised lowercase English letter.[10] For example, in figure 7 the last word of verse 17 has

8. Mandelkern's concordance verifies the correctness of this number; see Solomon Mandelkern, *Veteris Testamenti Concordantiae* (Tel Aviv: Schocken, 1971), 457. The other references where מִיָּד or יָד is spelled defectively are Lev. 9:22; 16:21; Ezek. 43:26; Job 5:18. The full Masoretic notations of Kethiv-Qere in these instances maintain that the word is to be read as "his hands" rather than "his hand," which would likewise use the consonants יד but would point the *wāw* with a *ḥôlem*: יָדוֹ.

9. Ibid., 972, 1179.

10. On occasion, a note in the textual apparatus refers to some feature that is not part of the text per se; e.g., the note (*BHS*, 1087) indicating the number of Psalm 1 is lacking in the Leningrad Codex.

a note in the apparatus (box E). Two or more words in the text that are discussed as a group in the apparatus are bracketed by the same raised lowercase letter—the first raised letter preceding the first word of the group and the second following the last word of the group. In figure 7, verse 22 has an example of this kind of note: the four words הָעָם כִּי בְרַע הוּא are preceded and followed by a raised *a* and are discussed as a group in the textual note that gives a variant reading for these four words according to the Septuagint. In this case, the third word of the group (בְרַע) also receives comment in the textual apparatus in a separate note (indicated by the letter *b*).

When a raised letter precedes the first word of a verse and the same letter is not repeated later in the same verse, the note in the textual apparatus refers to the entire verse (an example of this kind of note is found in verse 16 of figure 6). Two vertical lines separate different textual notes in the apparatus, and notes for a subsequent verse are introduced by a bold verse number (raised letters for a new verse begin with the letter *a*).[11] Notes that refer to a subsequent chapter are introduced by a bold **Cp**, followed by the chapter and verse number in bold (see the bottom of box F in figure 6). A single textual note may sometimes be indicated by a combination of two letters. In Psalm 1:1 (*BHS*, 1087), notes a and b are combined in the textual apparatus because the note refers to an inversion of the order of two elements of the Hebrew text as it is represented in the Syriac. Finally, a single letter may on occasion refer to two or more words of a single verse. In Exodus 34:14 (*BHS*, 144) the letter *a* is used for three words in succession: a verb, a noun, and an adjective. The note indicates that in each of the three cases the Septuagint reads a plural rather than a singular.

Two major difficulties are involved in reading the textual apparatus of *BHS*. First, a number of symbols refer to a variety of manuscripts and printed editions from which variants are cited. Other symbols characterize the kind of variant infor-

---

11. An exception to this practice is sometimes found when a series of textual notes refers to more than a single verse. For example, in the textual register that coincides with Num. 3:16–17, note a refers to verse 16, note b–b refers to three words that bridge the verse separator (i.e., the last word of verse 16 and the first two words of verse 17), and note c refers to a word in verse 17.

mation presented. A full list of these symbols may be found in
BHS (xliv–l). For the purposes of this book, an abbreviated list
of these symbols can be found in table 9.

TABLE 9   SYMBOLS USED IN *BHS*

Symbol	Meaning
ɯ	Samaritan Pentateuch
α′	Aquila's Greek version
ε′	Origen's Greek revision
θ′	Theodotion's Greek version
ο εβρ′	Origen's Hebrew text
σ′	Symmachus's Greek version
ᴜ	Arabic version
ʒ	Bomberg edition (ben Hayyim)
Bo	Bohairic version (Coptic)
C	Cairo Codex of the Prophets
ℭ	Hebrew fragments from Cairo Geniza
Ed(d)	Hebrew editions according to Kennicott, de Rossi, Ginsburg
𝕲	the Septuagint
Hier	Jerome
K	Kethiv
L	Leningrad Codex
𝕷	Old Latin (Itala)
𝔐	Masoretic Text
Mm	Masorah magna
Mp	Masorah parva
Ms(s)	Medieval Hebrew manuscript(s) according to Kennicott, de Rossi, Ginsburg
Occ	Western Masoretes
Or	Eastern Masoretes
Orig	Origen
Q	Qere
𝕼	Qumran manuscripts
ꜱ	Syriac (Peshitta)

TABLE 9 SYMBOLS USED IN *BHS* (cont'd.)

Symbol	Meaning
Sa	Sahidic version (Coptic)
ᵮ	Targums
Tiq soph	Tiqqun sopherim
ꭒ	Latin Vulgate
+	it adds, they add
>	is omitted, is missing

A second source of difficulty in reading the textual apparatus in *BHS* is that the text of the apparatus is written in an abbreviated form of Latin. Several works are available to help the beginning student deal with the Latin text of the *BHS* apparatus.[12]

Finally, it will be helpful to survey the general kinds of textual notes that appear in *BHS*. In the first place, many notes serve only to cite some peculiarity or idiosyncrasy of the Leningrad Codex. These notes may be of two types: those related to accents (Ps. 2:2, note b; Ps. 5:10, note c), and those related to differences in vocalization (Exod. 35:32, note a).

Next, there are notes about Hebrew manuscripts or ancient versions that offer an alternate reading. The simplest of these gives an alternate reading for a word or words in the text (Exod. 32:19, notes a and b; see figure 7).[13] Others give a word or words that a manuscript or version adds to the text (Exod. 32:18, notes a and b; see figure 7). Yet others indicate that a word or words of the Hebrew text are missing in certain manuscripts or versions (Exod. 32:29, note c; see figure 7).

Finally, some notes give the editor's suggestion for a certain text (the editor in these cases is the individual who was

---

12. The least extensive is Hans Peter Rüger, *An English Key to the Latin Words and Abbreviations and the Symbols of Biblia Hebraica Stuttgartensia* (Stuttgart: German Bible Society, 1985). (An adaptation of Rüger's work is found in the appendix to this volume.) More extensive and helpful are Wonneberger, *Understanding BHS*; Scott, *Simplified Guide to BHS*; and Würthwein, *Text of the Old Testament*.

13. On occasion, these alternate readings represent mere grammatical variation. In other cases, the variants involve differences in meaning.

responsible for the preparation of a particular section of *BHS*; see page ii for a list of editors). The editor may suggest that a certain phrase is a gloss and should be deleted (Ps. 1:3, note b–b; Ps. 2:2, note a–a). In many of these instances, the editor's suggestion is unsupported by ancient manuscript evidence and the student will do well to mark the subjectivity of the suggestion.[14] A related type of editorial suggestion is found in poetic texts. Often a textual note will read "delete for metric reasons" (Ps. 5:4, note a). Since modern scholarship only imperfectly understands Hebrew meter, the beginning student of textual criticism will do well to ignore this type of note.

Conclusion

This chapter has dealt with the page format, the Masoretic notation, and the general characteristics of the textual apparatus of *BHS*. With this introduction, the reader should be prepared to begin to interact with the information that is given in the apparatus of *BHS*. The following chapters indicate what the student should do with that information.

14. This discussion anticipates the fuller discussion found in chapter 7.

Scribal Errors

The previous chapter provided an introduction to the format and textual apparatus of *BHS*. This chapter surveys the kinds of scribal errors that found their way into Old Testament manuscripts throughout the long period in which the text was copied by hand. These scribal mistakes have been grouped in various ways by different authors. The discussion that follows considers them under three different classes.

First, and perhaps of least relevance for the modern text critic, is the flaw caused by a physical defect in the scroll from which the scribe was copying.[1] Obviously, a smudge or a worm hole could affect the work of the scribe who was copying a marred scroll. Unfortunately, the modern text critic has no way of gathering information about such errors and no way of systematizing them by types. Since this kind of fault is not predictable, it will not be considered further in this chapter.

A second and more important class of textual corruption includes a whole series of unintentional errors introduced into ancient Old Testament manuscripts by the human frailties of the scribes.[2]

1. Ernst Würthwein, *The Text of the Old Testament*, trans. Erroll F. Rhodes (Grand Rapids: Eerdmans, 1979), 105.

2. Frederic Kenyon, *Our Bible and the Ancient Manuscripts*, 4th ed. (New York: Harper, 1941), 19–20. P. Kyle McCarter Jr., *Textual Criticism: Recovering the Text of the Hebrew Bible* (Philadelphia: Fortress, 1986), 22, describes ancient scribes as "after all, human beings. They were fallible, apt to make mistakes out of carelessness, laziness, stupidity, . . . fatigue, or general incompetency."

Finally, a third important category of errors is classed as intentional.[3] Such changes are generally much less frequent for the Old Testament than for some other ancient documents.

Unintentional Errors

Unintentional errors did not arise because of a scribe's conscious decision to change the text, but rather because of the human limitations of the scribe and the scribal process. Scribes were undoubtedly often tired when they came to the end of their day's activities. This tiredness, coupled with adverse working conditions (poor lighting, interruptions, etc.), would have made error-free copying a virtual impossibility. The characteristics of the texts that they copied from—such as carelessly drawn letters or crowding—would only have compounded the difficulties of their task.

The various kinds of unintentional errors can be grouped under four major headings: (1) errors influenced by the text the scribe was working from; (2) errors that resulted from the scribe's carelessness or tiredness; (3) errors that were caused by dictation and/or hearing; and (4) errors that originated in the scribe's mind.[4]

Errors Related to the Manuscript Being Copied

Among errors that are predominantly manuscript based some are directly related to the letter or word being copied by the scribe;[5] they are discussed in the next four subsections. Others have to do with the presence of nearby words and the

3. Kenyon, *Our Bible and the Ancient Manuscripts*, 21; Würthwein, *Text of the Old Testament*, 105.

4. The unintentional errors discussed below are based on the following works: Artur Weiser, *The Old Testament: Its Formation and Development*, trans. Dorothea M. Barton (New York: Association Press, 1961), 355–57; Kenyon, *Our Bible and the Ancient Manuscripts*, 19–21; Aage Bentzen, *Introduction to the Old Testament* (Copenhagen: Gad, 1948), 1:98–99; Würthwein, *Text of the Old Testament*, 105–8; and McCarter, *Textual Criticism*, 26–61.

5. An analogous error should also be mentioned here, though it does not relate so much to the copying of Old Testament texts as to the translation of

effect of these words on a scribe copying a text; the final two
subsections describe errors of this second type.

Confusion of Similar Letters. One of the main sources of error that is directly related to the letter or word being copied is
the close similarity between certain pairs of Hebrew letters.
This likeness between letters, with its corresponding possibility for confused copying, applies to both the archaic script
(Phoenician) and the later square script (Aramaic). Letters
that could be easily confused in the archaic script include ב
and ד (Gen. 9:7), ב and ר (1 Kings 22:32), כ and מ (2 Kings
22:4), י and צ (Isa. 11:15), מ and שׁ (Num. 24:9), א and ד
(2 Chron. 22:10), א and ת (Num. 16:1), ל and נ (Job 15:35), and
נ and פ (1 Chron. 11:37, cf. 2 Sam. 23:35).[6]

Some consonants were susceptible to confusion in both the
archaic script and the later square script. These consonant
pairs include ר and ד and also ה and ח.[7] In the later Aramaic
script the consonant pairs that were subject to possible confusion included ב and כ (1 Chron. 17:20), י and ו (Isa. 30:4), ה
and ת (Exod. 34:19), and ח and ת (Ps. 49:15).[8]

---

the Old Testament into other languages. As is well known, the use of vowel
letters to indicate spelling was not carried out in a systematic way in the various stages of the writing and copying of the Old Testament. This means that
the translators of, say, the Septuagint, would have had to supply a particular
vowel tradition for the basically consonantal text that they were translating.
Due to the nature of the text, lacking a full written vowel indication, the
translators might have construed a word by incorrectly assigning a vowel
tradition to it. This kind of error is similar to those being discussed at this
point, but it relates more to the translation of the Old Testament than to its
transmission in Hebrew.

6. Bleddyn J. Roberts, *The Old Testament Text and Versions* (Cardiff: University of Wales Press, 1951), 92. Bentzen, *Introduction to the Old Testament*,
1:46, adds that מ and נ and ה and ח were also easily confused in the old script.
I do not suggest that all of these cases of letter confusion were equally probable nor that the examples given actually illustrate the confusion described.
In every textual difficulty there are a variety of more or less possible explanations for the state of the text. These lists of easily confused letters are given
as general background information that the text critic will use as part of an
arsenal of information with which to attack a particular textual problem.

7. Roberts, *Old Testament Text*, 93; and Bentzen, *Introduction to the Old
Testament*, 1:46.

8. Roberts, *Old Testament Text*, 93. Bentzen, *Introduction to the Old Testament*, 1:47, also lists ר and ד and ה and ח as susceptible to confusion in the
late script.

A classic example of confusion of letters involves a text that occurs in both Genesis 10:4 and 1 Chronicles 1:7. The Masoretic Text of Genesis 10:4 reads as follows: וּבְנֵי יָוָן אֱלִישָׁה וְתַרְשִׁישׁ כִּתִּים וְדֹדָנִים ("and the sons of Javan: Elishah and Tarshish, the Kittim and the Dodanim"). The textual apparatus of *BHS* for this verse indicates that some Hebrew manuscripts, the Samaritan Pentateuch, and the Septuagint all are in agreement with the text of 1 Chronicles 1:7, which reads רֹדָנִים instead of דֹדָנִים. It seems evident that a confusion of ד for ר or ר for ד has occurred in one of these texts. Many hold, rightly in my opinion, that רֹדָנִים is original because of a likely relation between the Rodanim and the Island of Rhodes.[9] In any case, whichever is the preferred spelling, a confusion of letters occurred in the transmission of one of the two words.

Wrong Word Division. Another kind of error that relates directly to the text from which a scribe copied is wrong word division. It was mentioned in chapter 2 that continuous writing was not practiced in writing Hebrew. Yet even though separation of words was practiced throughout the bulk of the Old Testament period, words would not always have been so carefully separated as they are in modern manuscripts and printed editions. This means that there was a potential for error in two directions. A scribe might unwittingly (but wrongly) combine two or more words into one word by careless crowding of his text. A Hebrew scribe might also wrongly separate a string of crowded consonants into words that were not the ones intended in the original form of the text. A well-known example in English is the unseparated phrase GODISNOWHERE, which may be separated to read either GOD IS NOW HERE or GOD IS NOWHERE.

As was mentioned in a previous chapter, the Septuagint was translated from a text that was written with word division indicated. Yet crowding in certain places of the *Vorlage* of the Septuagint may have caused the translators to err in judging where the word separations should have been. Some differ-

9. See, e.g., Derek Kidner, *Genesis* (Downers Grove, Ill.: InterVarsity, 1967), 106. Strangely, Herbert C. Leupold, *Exposition of Genesis* (Columbus: Wartburg, 1942; repr. Grand Rapids: Baker, 1960), 1:361–62, argues that דדנים is original and mentions that the Qere of 1 Chron. 1:7 reads דדנים, but a check of the Masorah in *BHS* indicates that this is not the case.

ences between the Septuagint and the Masoretic Text may be based on occasional incorrect division into words by the Septuagint translators.[10]

Bleddyn J. Roberts gives an example of wrong word division in Psalm 45:3 (v. 2 in English versions).[11] The first word of the verse in the Masoretic Text is יָפְיָפִיתָ, which *BHS* suggests should be read either as יָפוּ יָפִיתָ or יָפִי יָפִיתָ. This could be an example of wrong word division, but if it is, it is complicated by another factor: either simple haplography or a confusion of the letters ו and י then followed by haplography.

Wrong Assignment of Vowels. A third possible error related to the word a scribe was copying is an incorrect assignment of vowels. First, a scribe might have incorrectly placed a vowel letter in an early stage of the copying of the Hebrew text. Or he might have used a vowel letter that was ambiguous. Either error would have introduced a different form in the scribe's copy than the form of the text being copied. A more far reaching manner in which this kind of error could have affected the transmission of the text would have been in the stage of initial translation of the Hebrew into other languages (e.g., Greek). In fact, some suggest that the Septuagint translators understood the Hebrew vowel tradition less correctly than the scribes in mainstream Jewish circles did.[12]

Abbreviations. Misunderstood abbreviations could lead to a fourth kind of copying error. Some deny the use of abbreviations in the transmission of the Old Testament text, but Roberts insists that they must be considered as a potential source of error.[13] Common misinterpretations could arise from the use of י or ה for the divine name יהוה, as well as עד for the

10. Laird Harris (personal communication) suggests that had the *Vorlage* of the Septuagint been a text completely written in continuous fashion, one would expect many more evidences of incorrect word division than is the case. He holds that word crowding is a sufficient explanation for the cases of wrong word division that have been postulated for certain Septuagint–Masoretic Text differences.

11. Roberts, *Old Testament Text*, 93.

12. See, e.g., James Barr, *Comparative Philology and the Text of the Old Testament* (Oxford: Clarendon, 1987), 207–8.

13. Roberts, *Old Testament Text*, 97. See also two articles by Godfrey R. Driver: "Abbreviations in the Massoretic Text," *Textus* 1 (1960): 112–31; and "Once Again Abbreviations," *Textus* 4 (1964): 76–94.

phrase עַל־דְּבַר. In the first case, ה standing for the divine name could have been incorrectly attached to the end of the preceding word or to the beginning of the following word. The seeming preposition עַד ("unto") may actually refer to the phrase עַל־דְּבַר ("because of"; lit., "according to the word of") in Joshua 17:14.[14]

Homoeoteleuton. The preceding mistakes were related to the specific letter or word that the scribe was copying. But there were also errors that depended on the influence of neighboring words. The most important of these is known by the technical term *homoeoteleuton.* The term means "similar ending," and the fault is produced by the close presence in a particular context of words that are either identical or similar in their spelling at the end of the word.[15] The mechanism that accounts for the visual blunder is that the scribe's eye skips from the first occurrence of the word to its second, and the result is the omission of everything in between. An example of homoeoteleuton is found in the wording of Leviticus 4:25 (*BHS*, 162) in a copy found in the Cairo Geniza. Each half of the verse should end with the words מִזְבַּח הָעֹלָה, but the particular Cairo Geniza fragment cited omits the last half, a total of seven words. Apparently a scribe copied the first half of the verse but returned to looking at the last words of the verse in the manuscript he was copying and went on from there.[16]

Homoeoarkton. A related class of scribal oversight that is also influenced by the surrounding words is known by the technical name *homoeoarkton,* meaning "similar beginning." Examples of this kind of error are rarer than examples of homoeoteleuton.[17] The potential blunder is very similar to the preceding; the only difference is that the similar beginnings of two words or sets of words causes the skip and resulting omission of material. A probable example is found in the text

14. Roberts, *Old Testament Text,* 97; cf. BDB, 184.
15. Würthwein, *Text of the Old Testament,* 107.
16. It should be added that the words need not be totally identical for homoeoteleuton to occur. Leviticus 26:13 (*BHS*, 204) appears to offer a case where the cause of omission of three words from a Cairo Geniza copy is the partial similarity between the words עבדים and מצרים, an example that also includes confusion of ד and ר.
17. Würthwein, *Text of the Old Testament,* 107.

of Leviticus 17:10–12 (*BHS*, 188) in one of the Cairo Geniza fragments. Verses 10 and 13 of Leviticus 7 both begin with the pair of words אִישׁ אִישׁ. Apparently the scribe responsible for this manuscript copied the two words from verse 10, but then his eyes skipped to the same words in verse 13, and he continued copying, with the result that his copy omitted all of verses 10–12.

Errors Related to the Scribe's Fallibility

The use of a category entitled "scribe's fallibility" is not meant to imply that scribal fallibility had no role in the groups of errors treated above and below. It simply means that the scribe's fallibility seems to play the major role in the failures to be discussed immediately below. There are three types of errors in this category: haplography, dittography, and transposition (metathesis).

Haplography. Haplography refers to the inadvertent failure to write a letter(s) or word(s) that should appear in the text. In its simplest form, haplography is the copying once of a letter that was written twice in the text from which the scribe copied. A possible example of this mechanism is illustrated by the text of Deuteronomy 20:6–7 in fragments from the Cairo Geniza. Deuteronomy 20:5 (*BHS*, 322) ends with the imperfect verb יַחְנְכֶנּוּ and verse 6 begins with וּמִי. However, a Cairo Geniza fragment omits the connective ו at the start of verse 6. Remembering that verse numbers are a recent innovation, it is easy to postulate a haplography in the Cairo Geniza fragment. The end of verse 6 and the beginning of verse 7 offer an identical case.

An example of haplography of two words may be observed in Numbers 14:34 (*BHS*, 238), although the loss of the two words could also be explained as a case of homoeoteleuton (or even homoeoarkton). The Masoretic Text has a four-word sequence יוֹם לַשָּׁנָה יוֹם לַשָּׁנָה ("a day for a year, a day for a year"), but some medieval manuscripts contain יוֹם לַשָּׁנָה only once instead of twice.

Dittography. If haplography is writing once what should have been written twice, dittography is its exact opposite. The anomalous form in 2 Kings 15:16, הֶהָרוֹתֶיהָ (a noun with both the definite article and a suffix; *BHS*, 648), is probably to be explained as a dittograph of the initial ה of the word.[18] A more extensive possible dittograph is found in Leviticus 20:10 (*BHS*, 192). It is possible that the words אִישׁ אֲשֶׁר יִנְאַף אֶת־אֵשֶׁת ("a man who commits adultery with a woman") (bracketed by a–a in *BHS*) were not in the original form of the text, but may have been added by a dittograph of all but the initial ו of the first five words of the verse. Of course, it is also possible that the repeated words were primary and serve to express emphasis.

Transposition (Metathesis). A final kind of error in which the fallibility of the human scribe played the major role is transposition. This refers to the accidental reversing of two consonants in the copying of a word. This activity is present even on the lexical level in the Old Testament (e.g., the alternation of the two words for lamb in Hebrew: כֶּבֶשׂ and כֶּשֶׂב), and it is also present quite regularly in the area of textual criticism. A case in Numbers 15:35 (*BHS*, 241)—where the Masoretic Text has the infinitive absolute רָגוֹם and the Samaritan Pentateuch has the imperative רִגְמוּ—may involve only an interchange of the final two letters.[19] A second example of metathesis is found in Numbers 32:24 (*BHS*, 275), where the Masoretic Text reads לְצֹנַאֲכֶם, but more than twenty Hebrew manuscripts and the Samaritan Pentateuch read לְצֹאנְכֶם. The only difference between these two forms at the consonantal level is the interchange between נ and א. Examples of metathesis could be multiplied, but those mentioned should be sufficient for illustrative purposes.[20]

Errors Related to Dictation/Faulty Hearing

The errors discussed up to this point all involve problems of the scribe's vision and copying based on *seeing* a manu-

18. Roberts, *Old Testament Text*, 94–95.

19. If this is the accepted mechanism it implies that the change must have occurred before full vocalization and before the differentiation of final and medial forms of letters like מ (ם).

20. Laird Harris (personal communication) points out an interesting example in 2 Chron. 3:4 (*BHS*, 1516), the Masoretic Text of which reads מֵאָה וְעֶשְׂרִים ("one hundred and twenty"), but מֵאָה is almost surely an error by metathesis for אַמָּה ("cubit"). Cf. the note in the New International Version.

script. But there are also errors in the transmission of the Old
Testament text that are evidently based not on problems of *vision* and copying, but on problems of *hearing* and copying.
Apparently, at least on some occasions, Hebrew scribes copied on the basis of someone else's reading a manuscript
aloud. An example in English will illustrate this type of error:
"You can see for miles" and "You can see four miles." There
may be a slight difference in accent in the two sentences, but
it is easy to see how a listener could err in copying dictation
of one or the other of these two sentences.

Certain errors are best explained as errors of hearing. For
example, the interchange of guttural letters in some texts and
the mixing of certain sibilant sounds (principally ס and שׁ) are
probably based on errors in dictation and hearing.[21] Certain
other kinds of errors are usually attributed to this same mechanism. The negative particle לֹא and the preposition with
third-person masculine singular suffix לוֹ are virtually indis-
tinguishable when read aloud. To be sure, the context will often dictate which is meant, but there are still places where
both make good sense. An example of this difficulty is found
in Psalm 100:3 (*BHS*, 1180), where the Kethiv has לֹא and the
Qere לוֹ. In this case, both the Kethiv and the Qere make good
sense and either can be defended as the best reading.

Errors of the Scribe's Judgment

The last kind of unintentional error that scribes could have
introduced into the text they were copying is not related to
problems of sight or sound. Rather it develops because of a
scribe's misjudgment. These are still considered unintentional errors because they did not arise from a scribe's conscious decision to alter the text, but only from a lapse in his
thinking pattern. There are three different ways that a scribe
could alter a text by misjudgment.

First, a scribe could lapse into copying from mistaken
memory instead of actually copying from the exemplar. This
was all the more possible when the scribes knew their texts

21. Roberts, *Old Testament Text*, 96–97. For difficulties in the differentiation of the gutturals, note the confusion of the prepositions אֶל and עַל; cf.
Bentzen, *Introduction to the Old Testament*, 1:99.

very well. Certainly this would often have been the case with Jewish scribes and their intimate knowledge of the Old Testament text.[22]

A somewhat related error is seen when a scribe inadvertently made a text conform to a parallel reading. This, again, would be all the more likely with scribes who knew their material well.[23] This sort of blunder would need to be considered especially in those areas of the Old Testament that have extensive parallel passages (e.g., Samuel–Kings and Chronicles, certain Psalms, and the triple account of Hezekiah's reign found in Kings, Chronicles, and Isaiah).

A last kind of inadvertent error of judgment is found in those cases where a scribe may have incorporated a marginal reading or explanatory note from the exemplar into the new manuscript.[24] Here belong the so-called conflate or double readings where two readings are combined into one.[25] This particular class of error may well be borderline between the categories of unintentional and intentional changes.[26] In any specific text where a conflate reading is suspected, the text critic will have to determine, where possible, if the reading developed because of a scribe's inadvertent alteration or if it was an intentional change.

Intentional Changes

In this final section of the chapter the focus will be on intentional changes, that is, on those changes that were consciously introduced into the Old Testament text by the scribes. There are four kinds of intentional changes: *tiqqune sopherim* (emendations of the scribes), *itture sopherim* (omissions of the scribes), explanatory glosses, and substitution of euphemisms for what were thought to be vulgar or indelicate

22. Kenyon, *Our Bible and the Ancient Manuscripts*, 19–20.
23. Ibid.
24. Bentzen, *Introduction to the Old Testament*, 1:99.
25. Shemaryahu Talmon, "The Textual Study of the Bible—A New Outlook," in *Qumran and the History of the Biblical Text*, ed. Frank M. Cross and Shemaryahu Talmon (Cambridge: Harvard University Press, 1975), 344–50.
26. Bentzen, *Introduction to the Old Testament*, 1:99.

expressions in the original text.[27] (Some aspects of these kinds of changes were discussed previously in chapter 2, but they will be dealt with below in somewhat more detail.)

Emendations of the Scribes

The emendations of the scribes (*tiqqune sopherim*) are referred to in the Masorah and in various places in the Talmud. Tradition has it that in eighteen places the scribes altered the text because they thought that the original wording was disrespectful to God. An example is the text of Habakkuk 1:12, the Masoretic Text of which is translated, "Are you not from of old, Yahweh, my God, my Holy One? We will not die." According to the scribal tradition, the text originally stated that "you [Yahweh] will not die." Christian D. Ginsburg argues from the parallelism and from the Targum rendering that this is the clear meaning of the passage, but apparently the scribes' sensibilities would not allow them to let the text stand as written.[28]

There is some uncertainty in regard to these particular changes. In the first place, there is a variation in the lists of the places where these emendations or corrections of the scribes have been made. As mentioned above, tradition mentions eighteen places. In Ginsburg's classic work there is a list of sixteen texts in the Old Testament that were supposedly altered: Genesis 18:22; Numbers 11:15; 12:12; 1 Samuel 3:13; 2 Samuel 16:12; 20:1; Jeremiah 2:11; Ezekiel 8:17; Hosea 4:7; Habakkuk 1:12; Zechariah 2:12; Malachi 1:13; Psalm 106:20;

---

27. Some scholars include harmonizations under intentional changes; see Emanuel Tov, *Textual Criticism of the Hebrew Bible* (Minneapolis: Fortress, 1992), 261–62. While it is true that early scribes in the proto-Masoretic tradition may have occasionally harmonized the text in ways analogous to the harmonizations found in the Samaritan Pentateuch and certain Qumran texts, I have chosen not to include these in my treatment here because detecting their presence in the proto-Masoretic tradition is much harder than in the Samaritan Pentateuch (that is, no pristine form of the text can be used to identify harmonizations in the Masoretic Text). In my judgment, harmonizations in the Masoretic Text fall in the area of higher criticism.

28. Christian D. Ginsburg, *Introduction to the Massoretico-Critical Edition of the Hebrew Bible* (London: Trinitarian Bible Society, 1897; reprinted with prolegomenon by Harry M. Orlinsky: New York: Ktav, 1966), 358.

Job 7:20; 32:3; and Lamentations 3:20.[29] A check of *BHS* shows that all of these are indicated in the apparatus except for the two in 2 Samuel. Ernst Würthwein suggests that the eighteen cases mentioned by tradition are only a representative list and not meant to be exhaustive.[30]

A second uncertainty relates to the time when these supposed changes were made. The traditional name, emendations of the scribes (*tiqqune sopherim*), suggests that the changes were made some time between the time of Ezra and the tannaitic rabbis, that is, between the beginning of the fourth century B.C. and the first century A.D. But this assignment of the origin of the supposed changes was not universally accepted by talmudic authorities, nor is it totally accepted today. Some text critics, both ancient and modern, argue that the present wording in these texts is the preferred and that the material relating to the *tiqqune sopherim* is to be understood as midrashic interpretation and not textual history.[31]

Given these uncertainties, what can be said to summarize the state of the Hebrew text with regard to this type of intentional change? First, the changes, if in fact they are to be credited to the scribes, are not numerous. There may be some doubt about the exact number of these changes, but they do not represent an unknown amount of textual uncertainty. The number of such cases is some definite and rather small number. Second, that tradition speaks of these changes, albeit in sometimes conflicting numbers, indicates that these scribal emendations are to be viewed as something exceptional. The modern student of the Old Testament should be aware of this tradition, but they are not of critical importance in most of the Old Testament. They simply need to be considered in the case of those texts where they are supposed to have been made. The unintentional changes that were described earlier are of much more importance to the text critic for establishing the text of the Old Testament.

29. Ibid., 352–61.

30. Würthwein, *Text of the Old Testament*, 18. See also Carmel McCarthy, *The Tiqqune Sopherim* (Göttingen: Vandenhoeck & Ruprecht, 1981).

31. Israel Yeivin, *Introduction to the Tiberian Masorah*, trans. and ed. E. John Revell (Missoula, Mont.: Scholars Press, 1980), 50–51.

Omissions of the Scribes

The omissions of the scribes (*itture sopherim*) are, like the emendations of the scribes, mentioned in talmudic sources. These sources indicate that scribes made alterations in a total of seventeen passages in the Old Testament. Five of the cases have to do with the omission of a ו: Genesis 18:5; 24:55; Numbers 31:2; Psalm 36:7; 68:26. In a further seven cases words are read even though there are no consonants in the text: 2 Samuel 8:3; 16:23; Jeremiah 31:38; 50:29; Ruth 2:11; 3:5, 7. Finally, in five passages, words that are represented with consonants in the text are not read: 2 Kings 5:18; Jeremiah 32:11; 51:3; Ezekiel 48:16; and Ruth 3:12.[32] This means that in modern editions these consonants appear with no vowels. Both of the latter two types are illustrated in the textual commentary on the Book of Ruth that is the subject of chapter 8.

As in the case of the emendations of the scribes, so with the omissions of the scribes, the text critic is dealing with a definite number of cases that is relatively small. The student of text criticism needs to know something of the cases so as to deal with them when they occur in the text. But for the bulk of Old Testament text-critical work this type of intentional change need not occupy center stage.

Explanatory Glosses

It is at this stage that a fair amount of subjectivity enters the picture. It was mentioned above that the dividing line between unintentional and intentional changes of this type is difficult to fix. In addition, what for one text critic is a gloss will be part of the original text for another. The student of text criticism will need to judge the validity of arguments presented in critical commentaries for the alleged presence of glosses in the text. One observation should be stressed at this point. The obvious aim of all biblical writers was to communicate with their readers. This should serve to temper somewhat the urge to discover and remove explanatory glosses. At least some phrases that are said to be glosses may

32. Würthwein, *Text of the Old Testament*, 19. See further chapter 2.

in fact have been part of the original text of the Old Testament.[33]

Euphemisms

A final class of intentional changes is observed in sixteen places in the Old Testament text.[34] These are a special class of Kethiv-Qere readings in which the Kethiv was judged to be indelicate or offensive. The text was therefore changed by means of the Qere to a less offensive word or words. In addition to the Ishbaal/Ishbosheth interchange mentioned in chapter 2, an example is Isaiah 13:16, where the prophet, speaking in a judgment oracle about Babylon, says, "Their children will be dashed in pieces before them; their houses will be plundered, and their wives will be raped," a translation based on the Masoretic Text, specifically the Kethiv תִּשָּׁגַלְנָה ("will be raped"). The Qere in this case is תִּשָּׁכַבְנָה ("will be lain with"), an expression evidently viewed as less offensive than the Kethiv and thus substituted for it. Israel Yeivin cites the Babylonian Talmud, *Megilla* 25b, which says that "wherever the text is written indelicately, we read it delicately."[35]

Conclusion

This chapter has described the scribal errors that found their way into the text of the Old Testament throughout its

---

33. Michael Fishbane discusses glosses in a chapter entitled "Lexical and Explicative Comments" in *Biblical Interpretation in Ancient Israel* (Oxford: Clarendon, 1985), 44–65. His discussion is very valuable, especially in emphasizing the difficulties inherent in identifying glosses. On page 64 he summarizes the fourfold basis for discovering glosses: the use of deictic elements (pronouns such as הוּא, הִיא, etc.), inner-biblical parallels, variant text versions of a given passage, and "a cautious recognition of disruptive redundancies where these are also explanatory in nature." Even where there is explicit use of deictic elements in a passage, there still remains a large amount of subjectivity in determining whether a particular phrase is the work of the author (compiler) or of a later scribe. In many (most?) cases, the identification of glosses belongs more to the area of higher criticism than textual criticism.

34. Yeivin, *Tiberian Masorah*, 56.

35. Ibid.

transmission. These errors are of three kinds: accidental (i.e., physical deterioration of the manuscript being copied), unintentional, and intentional.[36] Only the errors of the latter two types are important for the study of the text of the Old Testament. When students analyze a particular textual problem, they should identify the probable types of errors that were responsible for the development of forms, a point that will be explored more fully in the following chapter.

36. The emphasis in this chapter has been on relatively small changes. These small changes represent the majority of text-critical work. The reader should be aware, however, that in certain books the differences between the Masoretic Text and, say, the Septuagint are major. In the case of Jeremiah, the Masoretic Text and the Septuagint probably represent different editions of the book; see Tov, *Textual Criticism of the Hebrew Bible*, 319–27. In my view, the determination of Jeremiah's two editions is mainly a concern of higher (or literary) criticism and not principally of textual criticism.

7

Principles and Practice
of Textual Criticism

Previous chapters have dealt principally with the history of the transmission of the Old Testament text, the arrangement and features of *BHS*, and the kinds of errors that are typically found in various manuscripts and editions of the Old Testament. This chapter will focus on how this background information is to be used in determining the original text. As mentioned in the introduction, the focus of Old Testament text criticism is different from the practice of text criticism of the New Testament or of classical Greek or Roman authors. In the New Testament the emphasis is on the study of variant readings, but Old Testament text criticism deals principally with perceived textual difficulties. Concerning this latter point, James Barr states:

> The reader finds "a difficulty" in the text which he is reading. He feels that it "does not make sense." The grammar is "wrong," i.e. does not fit with usual patterns of usage. The use of words is anomalous. Or perhaps the text contradicts what is said elsewhere in the same literary work. . . . These are simple examples of what is a "difficulty."[1]

This chapter has four main parts, each concerning a major step in the text-critical process. First, there is the preliminary step of gathering information for the perceived textual diffi-

1. James Barr, *Comparative Philology and the Text of the Old Testament* (Oxford: Clarendon, 1968), 3.

culties. All known variants for the passage in question have to be assembled. Second, the variant readings are grouped and evaluated, based on both external and internal evidence. In the third place, the text critic must select the best reading—the one that has the strongest claim to be the original reading—from the various possibilities that are attested in ancient sources.[2] Finally, in those cases where there appears to be no attested reading that makes any sense, the text critic may have to resort to conjectural emendation.

Before dealing with these four areas it will be helpful to illustrate how the work of the text critic can result in the determination of the original form(s) of a text. Figure 8 reflects a hypothetical *Urtext* and the variable relationship between it and three primary textual witnesses: the Masoretic Text, the Septuagint, and the Samaritan Pentateuch.[3] It will be noted that *no* single witness reproduces fully and faithfully the wording of the *Urtext* and that the critic has no direct recourse to the *Urtext* (the only access the critic has to the *Urtext* is through the varying testimony of known forms of the text). It should also be evident that there are various possible situations of agreement and disagreement between the three witnesses.[4] By careful study of the variations that exist in the wording of the three witnesses, the text critic can, at least theoretically, postulate the form of the *Urtext*. The rest of the chapter will seek to fill in the details of the way that the text critic should go about this work.

2. In synoptic passages more than a single reading may well be original. See Bruce K. Waltke, "Aims of OT Textual Criticism," *Westminster Theological Journal* 51 (1989): 102–7.

3. Each of these three witnesses could contain variant readings as well. The situation is simplified in the diagram for ease of comprehension.

4. The possibilities represented are (1) agreement between all three witnesses (case *a*); (2) agreement of two witnesses against a third (*b, c, d*); (3) and disagreement between all three witnesses (*e*). In the second scenario (*b, c, d*), a minority witness could preserve the reading of the *Urtext*, but this is not illustrated in the diagram. In case *e*, it might be that one witness still represents the reading of the *Urtext*. In figure 8, however, case *e* represents the need for conjectural emendation since none of the attested readings makes good sense in the context.

FIGURE 8   URTEXT

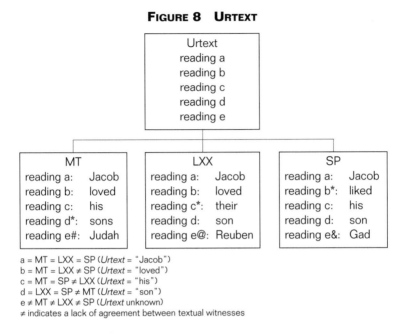

a = MT = LXX = SP (*Urtext* = "Jacob")
b = MT = LXX ≠ SP (*Urtext* = "loved")
c = MT = SP ≠ LXX (*Urtext* = "his")
d = LXX = SP ≠ MT (*Urtext* = "son")
e ≠ MT ≠ LXX ≠ SP (*Urtext* unknown)
≠ indicates a lack of agreement between textual witnesses

Collection of Evidence

Since the purpose of this book is to help begin the text-critical process, the collection of evidence will be limited in scope to that presented in the apparatus of *BHS*. The more advanced student will be able to apply the procedures outlined here, but will need to augment the data supplied in *BHS* by checking the critical editions of the various texts and versions.

For a given text, then, the student or pastor will need to decipher and write out the variants listed in the *BHS* apparatus for the verse or passage that is the object of study (symbols used in the *BHS* apparatus are explained in its introduction, xliv–l).[5] In most cases this will include Hebrew variants and readings in the versions that may or may not reflect a variant

5. The student may need additional help to make use of the symbols used in *BHS*. Two works will probably be needed by the beginning text critic: Reinhard Wonneberger, *Understanding BHS: A Manual for the Users of Biblia*

in the Hebrew text on which the version was based. At this stage the student should write out in full all Hebrew variants listed and all potential versional variants. The versional variants should be retroverted (retranslated from the language of the version to their probable corresponding Hebrew forms). This is necessary even though at a later stage the student may decide that the difference lies with the version itself and not with the Hebrew *Vorlage*. An additional step before evaluating the variants is to translate all variants. This will allow the student of the text to make a preliminary evaluation of whether the textual variants are critical to exegesis or not.[6]

Evaluation of Variants

It is important to remember that textual criticism is both an art and a science.[7] This means that both subjective and objective elements enter into the process. Textual criticism is not exclusively a science because of the many limits to our knowledge of the history of the transmission of ancient texts. These limits imply that one's judgment about textual questions will necessarily be, at least in part, subjective. To say this is not to argue that textual criticism is completely subjective, however. Certain scientific principles serve as guides to those who work in textual matters. Several of these principles are also used in the textual criticism of other ancient documents, for example, the New Testament and classical Greek and Roman authors. In the next several paragraphs these principles will be described and discussed. As will be seen, these principles must be used together. The application of any one of them in isolation could lead to erroneous results.

Hebraica Stuttgartensia, trans. Dwight R. Daniels, 2d ed. (Rome: Pontifical Biblical Institute Press, 1990); and William R. Scott, *A Simplified Guide to BHS* (Berkeley: BIBAL, 1987).

6. See further the final evaluation of the importance of the variants under step three, "Selection of the Best Reading."

7. Cf. P. Kyle McCarter Jr., *Textual Criticism: Recovering the Text of the Hebrew Bible* (Philadelphia: Fortress, 1986), 11. McCarter titles an entire chapter "The Art and Science of Textual Criticism."

The first step in evaluating the variant readings of a given passage has to do with external evidence. There is a difference of opinion among Old Testament text critics with regard to external evidence. Some give greater value to the readings of the Masoretic Text and less value to any of the readings of the various versions. Others argue that the Masoretic Text is only one of several witnesses to the wording of the text and should not be considered more valuable than any other.[8] In the light of what has been said in chapters 1 and 2, the absolute superiority of the Masoretic Text in every verse of the Old Testament cannot be maintained. But neither should the Masoretic Text be relegated to being just one more witness to the wording of the text. As a whole, the Masoretic Text is certainly to be valued more highly than the witness derived from the versions. But in any one particular text, the various readings of all witnesses must be considered and a valid decision reached based on internal evidence.[9]

What then are the principles of internal evidence?[10] P. Kyle McCarter suggests that the primary principle of textual criticism has to do with determining which reading could most plausibly have given rise to the others.[11] Based on the mechanisms discussed in chapter 7, certain original readings may have given rise to changes along well-known lines leading to

8. These positions are somewhat simplified to highlight the contrast between two differing approaches. In practice, few text critics would adopt either of the alternatives as expressed in this simplified form.

9. It is an error to convert a general truth ("on the whole the Masoretic Text is superior") into an absolute truth ("the Masoretic Text is always superior"). While it is true that the Masoretic Text is usually superior, the text critic must determine if it is actually superior or not in a particular text. McCarter, *Textual Criticism*, 71–72, speaks of external evidence as "unreliable." Yet he also speaks of the probability that the Masoretic Text generally preserves the better text. When he speaks of external evidence being unreliable, he seems to mean that external evidence by itself cannot determine the reading in any given Old Testament text. This is precisely the position that I have tried to maintain in this book.

10. Emanuel Tov, "Criteria for Evaluating Textual Readings: The Limitations of Textual Rules," *Harvard Theological Review* 75 (1982): 429–48, argues that the rules often used in textual criticism are of limited value. He does not advocate their abolishment, but only that the text critic recognize their limitations.

11. McCarter, *Textual Criticism*, 72.

secondary readings. In some cases, at least, the opposite changes may well have been impossible. Thus a knowledge of normal scribal tendencies may in many cases indicate the direction of a textual change. And once the direction of the change is known, the original reading can be determined. This principle will be illustrated in some of the examples treated in chapter 8.

A second general principle of internal evidence is that of the level of difficulty of two or more readings. In such cases, the "more difficult" reading (*lectio difficilior*) is to be preferred.[12] This principle is based on the tendency of scribes to simplify and clarify the texts that they were copying much more often than they would have made them more difficult. The principle is valid, but it must be used in conjunction with other principles, for there were scribal mistakes that did in fact make their text more difficult. As McCarter well states, "The more difficult reading is not to be preferred when it is garbage."[13]

A third principle of internal evidence relates to the length of two or more variant readings. In these cases, text critics often judge the shorter reading (*lectio brevior*) to be preferable and more likely original. This general judgment is based on the normal scribal tendency to amplify a text by adding words to clarify or smooth out the text. Of course this principle must not be used as an ironclad rule, for several of the common unintentional errors described in chapter 7 resulted in shorter texts. In cases, for example, of haplography, the shorter text is obviously not better (i.e., original).[14]

McCarter describes several additional principles for evaluating internal evidence.[15] In most respects these are not different principles, but are merely more specific examples of the principle of the more difficult reading. He lists, among

12. Ibid. See also Bruce K. Waltke, "The Textual Criticism of the Old Testament," in *The Expositor's Bible Commentary*, ed. Frank E. Gaebelein (Grand Rapids: Zondervan, 1979), 1:226.

13. McCarter, *Textual Criticism*, 73. Waltke, "Textual Criticism," 226, states that "a 'more difficult reading' does not mean a 'meaningless and corrupt reading.'"

14. McCarter, *Textual Criticism*, 74.

15. Ibid.

others, the appropriateness of a reading to its context, readings that resolve contradictions, and the special rule of parallel texts.[16] The reader should appreciate that there is the possibility of a large measure of subjectivity in using these last three principles. For example, readings that resolve contradictions should not be rejected absolutely. Other factors must be taken into account if the text critic is to avoid a large measure of subjectivity in his or her work. This serves as a good reminder that these principles must be used together and must be used with sensitivity in the text critic's work.

Selection of the Best Reading

This step is not so much a separate part of the text-critical work, but it is more a continuation of the previous step. It is listed separately to emphasize the importance of the procedure. The selection of the best reading will of course be based on the evidence assembled in the preceding step. In most cases, the evaluation of the evidence will point to one reading as most obviously the best or most original. The text critic's task at this point is to state that reading "x" is the best reading and to give the reasons for this decision. These reasons will include as full an explanation as possible for the probable development of the various secondary readings that are "competing" with the original reading. The explanation should clearly indicate why a particular reading is preferred and why the secondary readings are not to be viewed as original.

One small additional step is important at this point. The text critic should state clearly what difference the various readings would make for exegesis. The overall goal for the student of Scripture is to determine what the text says. Thus textual criticism must serve exegesis. In many cases the existence of variant readings is of little consequence for exegesis, even though all variant readings are important for the study of the transmission of the text. For example, cases of varied orthography (spelling) will often have little or no impact on exegesis. If this is the case, the text critic needs to

16. Ibid.

state this. If, on the other hand, one or more of the variants makes a major difference to exegesis, that too should be indicated. This final step of the selection of the best reading will allow the student of the text to get a better feeling for the overall state of the text than a mere solving of individual textual problems might offer. Perhaps it would even be advisable to categorize the textual problems of a given unit in their relation to exegesis: inconsequential, minor value, or major value. Such a procedure will allow the text critic to place major emphasis on the textual problems that will make the greatest impact on exegesis.

Emendation of the Text

Most of the time the preceding three steps will allow the student of the Old Testament text to resolve textual difficulties. But there are times when the process described above does not lead to a convincing solution. At least two kinds of situations can be visualized. First, there is the case of two or more readings that are equally plausible. While some would emend in this case, others would not.[17] I am of the conviction that emendation is not required or advisable in such situations. To paraphrase an old Spanish proverb—"a known evil is better than a good thing to be known"[18]—"evil" in the text-critical process speaks of an inability to determine the original reading. But a case of not knowing which of two or more attested readings is original is far better (in my opinion) than the "unknown evil" of suggesting an emendation that has no attestation in any manuscript tradition whatever. In other

17. Cf. McCarter, *Textual Criticism*, 74–75: "[Emendation] should be attempted whenever the text critic suspects that the primitive reading has not been preserved by any extant witness." For somewhat different advice, see Waltke, "Textual Criticism," 226: "Where Hebrew MSS and ancient versions offer good and sensible readings and a superior reading cannot be demonstrated on the basis of the above two rules, one should, as a matter of first principle, allow MT to stand."

18. The original version of this proverb reads, "Más vale malo conocido, que bueno por conocer." I thank Ignacio Simal Camps for checking the wording of this proverb.

words, it is better in these cases that exegesis rest on a plausible and attested reading than on no attested reading. A second kind of situation where emendation is used is the case of a text where no attested reading makes sense.[19] In such situations, emendation may be resorted to, but even there it must be used with caution. Bruce Waltke states the procedure for cases like these:

> One may attempt a conjecture concerning the true reading—a conjecture that must be validated by demonstrating the process of the textual corruption from the original to the existing text-forms. Such conjectures, however, can never be used to validate the interpretation of the whole passage in that they will have been made on the basis of an expectation derived from the whole.[20]

McCarter tells the text critic to ask two important questions when suggesting emendations: "Does the proposed emendation explain all the transmitted readings? Is it suited to its context?" If either of these questions must be answered "no," McCarter suggests that the textual problem must be declared "unsolved."[21]

Some text critics are much more willing to emend the vocalization of the Hebrew text than the consonantal text. While it is true that the age of the *written* vowels is much later than the age of the consonants, this in itself does not authorize the text critic to emend vowels more quickly than consonants. As was demonstrated in chapter 2, the Masoretic vowel signs were based on a carefully transmitted vowel tradition. It is my conviction that emendation of either vowels or consonants must be used only in cases where no other options are available. It is interesting to note that in recent decades there has

19. In some cases where both the Masoretic Text and the versions are difficult, the difficulty of the Masoretic Text may be explained by recourse to comparative philology (i.e., a difficult word or syntactical structure may be elucidated by information from one of the other Semitic languages). The interested reader should consult Barr, *Comparative Philology and the Text of the Old Testament*, esp. 1–3, where he develops the importance of the philological approach as a complement to the textual approach.

20. Waltke, "Textual Criticism," 226.

21. McCarter, *Textual Criticism*, 75.

been a change from a rather cavalier attitude toward emendations to a more conservative approach.[22]

Conclusion

This chapter has outlined a procedure for solving textual problems in the Old Testament. The variants must be collected, translated, and evaluated. The reading with the best evidence is chosen as the best reading and is most likely the original reading. In cases where no textual witness makes sense, the text critic may suggest an emendation. The following chapter will illustrate the use of these principles by examining the textual difficulties that are found in the Hebrew text of the Book of Ruth.

22. Ibid.

Textual Commentary on the Book of Ruth

The preceding chapter described principles used in the practice of Old Testament textual criticism. This chapter illustrates those principles through an examination of the textual problems in the Book of Ruth that are indicated in the critical apparatus of *BHS*. In each case the variants are listed and evaluated. My purpose in this chapter is more to illustrate the process of Old Testament textual criticism than to present a finished and definitive product of textual analysis. Where possible, therefore, more than one solution of a particular textual problem is suggested.[1]

Ruth 1:1

The first of two references to 1:1 in the textual apparatus of *BHS* is indicated by the repeated superscript letters *a–a*, which refer to the two words between them. The variants and translations for this note are as follows:

MT	בִּימֵי שְׁפֹט	now it happened in the days of the judging of the judges

1. The deciphering of the textual apparatus of *BHS* throughout this chapter is based on help provided by Reinhard Wonneberger, *Understanding BHS: A Manual for the Users of Biblia Hebraica Stuttgartensia*, trans. Dwight R. Daniels, 2d ed. (Rome: Pontifical Biblical Institute Press, 1990); and William R. Scott, *A Simplified Guide to BHS* (Berkeley: BIBAL, 1987). These two helps, however, will not be repeatedly cited throughout the chapter.

LXX*[2]	ἐν τῷ κρίνειν = בִּשְׁפֹט	now it happened when the judges judged
Syriac	omits שְׁפֹט	now it happened in the days of the judges

It should be obvious that the wording of the Masoretic Text here is somewhat cumbersome.[3] The Septuagint and the Syriac, *if* they both represent a Hebrew *Vorlage* that is different from the Masoretic Text, would each reflect a more normal Hebrew syntax. The Masoretic Text is arguably the best since it is the "more difficult" reading and since the Septuagint and Syriac show two different "corrections" of the syntax. Moreover there is no easily explained scribal mechanism for the insertion of the words in the Masoretic Text.

If the Hebrew texts from which the Septuagint and Syriac were translated were different from the Masoretic Text, they were probably the result of a smoothing out of the text by Jewish scribes. Alternatively, the smoothing out may have been done by the translators themselves or in subsequent revisions of the Greek or Syriac texts. While the Masoretic Text is to be preferred, it should be noted in this case that there is no essential change of meaning regardless of which variant is read. The variants relate only to usage or syntactical custom.[4] While the textual variants are interesting from the point of view of text transmission, they have no effect on exegesis.

The second note in Ruth 1:1 is indicated by the letter *b*. The variants indicated in the apparatus, and their translations, are as follows:

MT	וּשְׁנֵי בָנָיו	he and his wife and his two sons

2. The symbol ග* refers to the original Greek text, i.e., the unanimous reading of the various Greek manuscripts.

3. Edward F. Campbell Jr., *Ruth*, Anchor Bible 7 (Garden City, N.Y.: Doubleday, 1975), 49, calls the syntax of the five words that begin Ruth "unique." Jack M. Sasson, *Ruth: A New Translation with a Philological Commentary and a Formalist-Folklorist Interpretation* (Baltimore: Johns Hopkins University Press, 1979), 15, qualifies the grammar of this phrase as unusual.

4. Bruce K. Waltke (private communication) suggests that בִּימֵי is a quasi-prepositional phrase meaning "when." In his view, the Septuagint in this case does not indicate a different *Vorlage*.

LXX, (Syriac)[5] καὶ οἱ υἱοὶ αὐτοῦ[6] he and his wife and his sons

Since the Syriac agrees generally with the Septuagint it has not been listed separately in translation. In this case it is possible that a scribe at some point in the transmission of the Hebrew text added the word שְׁנֵי under the influence of the following verse (this would then be a harmonizing addition— either unconscious or intentional). But there is also the possibility that שְׁנֵי was inadvertently dropped at some point in the translation or revision of the Septuagint and Syriac.[7] At any rate, even though the difference is significant within the confines of 1:1, its overall significance in context is very slight. The presence or absence of שְׁנֵי in 1:1 has little impact on the meaning of the unit of text, 1:1–5. In terms of the classification of textual problems suggested in the last chapter, this problem should be classed as of minor importance for exegesis.

Ruth 1:8

For the Kethiv-Qere in 1:8 the Septuagint and Vulgate agree with the Qere, according to Theodore H. Robinson, the editor of this section of *BHS*. The readings are as follows:[8]

Kethiv	יַעֲשֶׂה
Qere	יַעַשׂ
LXX	ποιήσαι[9]
Vulgate	agrees with LXX and Qere

5. Parentheses around a version's siglum indicate that the version agrees with the basic issue under consideration, but does not necessarily agree in all details. In this case, the Syriac agrees with the Septuagint in the omission of the number *two*, but it does not agree with all features of the Septuagint.

6. Alan E. Brooke and Norman McLean (eds.), *The Old Testament in Greek*, vol. 1/4: *Joshua, Judges, and Ruth* (Cambridge: Cambridge University Press, 1917), 887.

7. It is possible that a scribe's (or translator's) eye skipped from the *wāw* of וּשְׁנֵי to the *yôd*, so copying (or translating) וּבְנֵיו rather than שְׁנֵי בָנָיו. This would then be a special case where homoeoarkton and homoeoteleuton are combined in a single word.

8. Note that the form printed in the text of *BHS* is a hybrid form. It has the consonants of the Kethiv but the vowels of the Qere.

9. Brooke and McLean, *Old Testament in Greek*, 888. The form is a third-person singular optative aorist active.

It is first necessary to distinguish between the Kethiv and the Qere forms: both are qal third-person masculine singular verbs; the Kethiv is imperfect and the Qere is jussive. The Kethiv may be translated as a simple future ("Yahweh will treat you with loyal love"), and this is the most usual translation of the imperfect. But it is not the only translation. The imperfect can also be used to express the wish or desire of a person,[10] in which case the translation would be the same as that of the Qere's jussive: "May Yahweh treat you with loyal love." This nuance is expressed with the identical imperfect form later in the chapter: כֹּה יַעֲשֶׂה יְהֹוָה לִי ("thus may Yahweh do to me") (1:17).

The ambiguity inherent in the Kethiv's two possible translations calls for a decision by the reader or exegete. It would appear that the ambiguity makes the Kethiv the more difficult reading, and as such it could have easily been "corrected" at some point in the transmission of the text, a correction that came to be represented in the unambiguous Qere.[11] This direction for the change is much more likely than the reverse (i.e., a scribe making an unambiguous text ambiguous).[12] The testimony of the Septuagint and Vulgate here does not mean that their translators necessarily read the Qere. They may have, but these translators may also have simply rendered the Kethiv according to the context.[13]

10. GKC, 317. Bruce K. Waltke and Michael O'Connor, *Introduction to Biblical Hebrew Syntax* (Winona Lake, Ind.: Eisenbrauns, 1990), 509–10, call this use a nonperfective of injunction.

11. I am not maintaining that every *Qere* is a correction of the Kethiv. See the previous discussion of Kethiv-Qere in chapter 2.

12. One could imagine that the present Kethiv represents a conflate reading. The letter ה might have been used as an abbreviation for the divine name; cf. Godfrey R. Driver, "Once Again Abbreviations," *Textus* 4 (1964): 79. At a subsequent stage a scribe corrected this to the full spelling of the divine name, and at a later stage yet another scribe produced a conflate reading and ה came to be associated with the previous verb form. While there is nothing inherently impossible with this explanation, it seems that the simplest explanation for a textual change should be accepted as a matter of principle.

13. It can be argued that Naomi's state of mind at this point in the narrative is much more consistent with the expression of a wish ("May Yahweh . . .") than with the expression of a promise ("Yahweh *will* do so and so . . ."). Presumably the scribe responsible for the Qere and the translators of the Septuagint and Vulgate understood this.

Since the Kethiv is capable of expressing what the Qere expresses, this textual difficulty should also be classed as of minor importance. If the Qere had expressed a meaning that the Kethiv could not express, then the textual problem would have been classed as having major importance for the exegesis of the passage.

Ruth 1:14

In 1:14[14] there is an addition in the Septuagint at the point marked by the letter *a*. The added text reads καὶ ἐπέστρεψεν εἰς τὸν λαὸν αὐτῆς. Robinson suggests that the Hebrew original perhaps read וַתָּשָׁב אֶל־עַמָּהּ at this point. The Masoretic Text and the Septuagint may be translated as follows:

MT   Orpah kissed her mother-in-law, but Ruth embraced her

LXX   Orpah kissed her mother-in-law and returned to her people, but Ruth followed her[15]

It is possible to understand the Septuagint as representing the preferred text. If this was the case, the Masoretic Text may be explained as having suffered an inadvertent loss due to homoeoteleuton (the last word preceding the lost phrase ends with ה, like the last word of the phrase). Since, however, the addition of the Septuagint expresses what is clearly implied in the Masoretic Text, it can also be argued that the Septuagint has made explicit what is implicit in the Masoretic Text.[16] This would be an example of the general principle that, other things being equal, the shorter reading is to be preferred as more likely primary. The Masoretic Text should be translated with sensitivity so as to capture the implied action of Orpah:

14. There is no indication in this verse of a Kethiv-Qere. Campbell's comment (*Ruth*, 71) that the Qere has א in the word וַתִּשֶּׂנָה is therefore puzzling. The Masorah parva for this word indicates that the Masoretes spelled the word in question twice without א.

15. It is interesting to note that the Septuagint translates literally the Hebrew idiom *they lifted up their voices and wept*.

16. This is the opinion of some older text critics such as Cappel, Buxtorf, and Clericus, as cited in Dominique Barthélemy, *Critique Textuelle de l'Ancien Testament*, Orbis Biblicus et Orientalis 50/1 (Göttingen: Vandenhoeck & Ruprecht, 1982), 130.

"Orpah kissed her mother-in-law goodbye, but Ruth embraced her (indicating a desire to stay)."[17] Here the text critic has a choice of two plausible explanations for the original text and the mechanism of its alteration.[18] In either case, the significance of the error for exegesis is minor.

Ruth 1:19

There are three references in the apparatus of *BHS* for 1:19. The first, marked by the letter *a*, refers to the pronominal suffix of the Masoretic Text's שְׁתֵּיהֶם. The note suggests that the text should read שְׁתֵּיהֶן with more than twenty medieval manuscripts (indicated by the abbreviation "mlt Mss"). The difference between these two forms is that the pronominal suffix in the Masoretic Text is third-person masculine plural, and in the medieval manuscripts it is third-person feminine plural.[19] In context, the suffix refers to Naomi and Ruth, and therefore the form of the medieval manuscripts is more "grammatically correct." Yet it is well known that a masculine plural suffix can refer to feminine antecedents.[20] It would appear that the unusual suffix of the Masoretic Text was "corrected" to the more usual form in some of the medieval Hebrew manuscripts. The issue here is not one of meaning or exegesis. All that is at issue is a grammatical custom regarding the use of pronominal suffixes.

The second note for 1:19 is marked by the letters *b–b*. Four words of the Masoretic Text, וַתְּהִי כְּבֹאָנָה בֵּית לֶחֶם, are omitted in the Septuagint. There is admittedly some redundancy in the wording of the Masoretic Text. One could perhaps argue for a kind of dittography here, but if so, it is dittography with some other complicating factor. It is not a simple case of dit-

17. Barthélemy, *Critique Textuelle*, 130, where the translation "kiss goodbye" is cited in several places in the Old Testament.

18. The choice between the two explanations will reflect the critic's overall understanding of text history and experience in the practice of text criticism. I believe it best here to leave the reader with the choice.

19. Campbell, *Ruth*, 65, 75, explains the form in the Masoretic Text as an ancient feminine dual suffix. He points out that this feature is found seven times in the Book of Ruth where the pronoun refers to both Naomi and Ruth, and he cites parallel examples from elsewhere in the Old Testament.

20. GKC, 440; Waltke and O'Connor, *Biblical Hebrew Syntax*, 108, 302.

tography, since the wording of the phrase is not identical to the preceding phrase in the Masoretic Text. It may be more plausibly argued that a scribe involved in copying the *Vorlage* of the Septuagint, or the translator of the Septuagint, omitted the words due to homoeoteleuton (both the omitted phrase and the phrase preceding it end with בֵּית לֶחֶם). Actually, the form of the Masoretic Text may express some kind of emphasis here by the repetition of certain words. All of this is admittedly subjective, and each text critic must make a choice as to the most likely wording of the original. What is germane to the purpose of this book is the illustration of how two of the principles given in the last chapter sometimes conflict. The Septuagint is the shorter reading, while the Masoretic Text is the more difficult reading. If the Masoretic Text is indeed emphatic in its repetition, this would tip the balance toward it as the primary reading.

The final variant recorded for 1:19 is marked by the letter *c*. In this case the testimony of the Septuagint is split between various manuscripts.[21] The variants are as follows:

MT	עֲלֵיהֶן
Vaticanus	ἐπ᾿ αὐτῆς
Alexandrinus, Marchalianus	αὐτῇ

The Greek variants are similar in meaning.[22] The major difference is between the plural pronominal suffix of the Masoretic Text and the singular pronoun in the various Septuagint manuscripts. The Masoretic Text indicates that "all the city was stirred up" over the arrival of the two women; the Septuagint indicates that the city was stirred up over Naomi's arrival. A check of the context shows that indeed the

21. This is a good reminder that the text of the Septuagint, or any version, must itself be subjected to textual criticism before it can be used for textual criticism of the Masoretic Text.

22. Not all Septuagint variants are listed in *BHS*. A check of Brooke and McLean, *Old Testament in Greek*, 889, indicates that four readings are attested: (επ) αυτης, αυτη, αυτας, and αυταις. The singular is probably the original Greek reading, whether genitive (object of ἐπί) or dative, since this reading is at variance with the Masoretic Text.

women of Bethlehem only spoke of Naomi in their dialogue. It could be argued that the Septuagint (or its *Vorlage*) adapted the pronoun to its subsequent context.

The reading of the Masoretic Text, however, agrees with the preceding references to the two women (e.g., "when they entered Bethlehem"). This reading may have been adjusted to these earlier references (the Masoretic Text may, in fact, be the easier reading). As it now stands, the Masoretic Text expresses a general reaction of "all the city" (i.e., all the inhabitants, an example of metonymy) to the arrival of the two women, one of whom was a Moabite. The following phrase expresses a more specific reaction of the women of Bethlehem to the arrival of Naomi, a woman that many of them would have known well before her sojourn in Moab. The change, whichever direction it may have occurred, is of some importance to exegesis.

Ruth 1:20

Robinson suggests following the reading of more then twenty medieval manuscripts: מָרָה versus the Masoretic Text's מָרָא. מָרָה is the more usual spelling for this Hebrew adjective, while מָרָא could reflect a typical spelling in Aramaic. The medieval copyists very likely changed the unusual spelling into the more usual. This is much more likely than the possibility that early scribes changed a usual spelling into an unusual one.[23] Sasson argues that the name is derived from a Hebrew root מרר, but not with the normal meaning "bitter." He holds that a secondary meaning is attested for this root: "to bless, strengthen."[24] Hubbard argues that the word play used by the author discounts the meaning suggested by Sasson. He derives the name from the root מרר and suggests that the final א is a diminutive ending.[25]

---

23. Campbell, *Ruth*, 76, argues that this form is not technically an Aramaism. He views it as possibly "only an orthographic change in the course of scribal transmission."

24. Sasson, *Ruth*, 32–33.

25. Robert L. Hubbard Jr., *The Book of Ruth*, New International Commentary on the Old Testament (Grand Rapids: Eerdmans, 1988), 122 n. 9. According to Hubbard, the name is not an Aramaism, since there is no Aramaic root to derive it from.

Ruth 1:21

The textual note for 1:21 is marked by the letters *a–a*.[26] The variants are as follows:

MT	עָנָה בִי
LXX	ἐταπείνωσέν με

The Syriac and Vulgate are in agreement with the Septuagint rendering, which can be translated, "He humbled me." The Septuagint appears to have read the same consonants as the Masoretic Text, but with a different vocalization: עִנָּה, a piel perfect from the root ענה III (cf. BDB, 776). The Masoretic Text reads a qal perfect, which could express a specialized meaning of the root ענה I. In the latter case, the text would be translated, "He testified against me"—a translation that is found in legal contexts.[27] Three considerations argue that the Masoretic Text is original. Hubbard suggests the possibility of a paronomastic word play between עָנָה בִי and נָעֳמִי.[28] In addition, as mentioned in chapter 2, the understanding that the translators of the Septuagint had of the vowel tradition of their Hebrew *Vorlage* was not as good as that within the mainstream Jewish scribal tradition. Third, there is a strong possibility that a rare use of a word could have more easily been changed into a normal use, but the opposite tendency is not so likely. The Septuagint translators, perhaps unsure of how the qal of ענה I would have fit into the context, could have easily substituted the meaning of the piel of ענה III in their translation. In my opinion, the Masoretic Text is preferred, and the text should be translated, "He testified against me," or perhaps, "He judged me."

---

26. The reader is reminded that there are more textual variants than those represented in the apparatus of *BHS*. For example, in 1:13 the Septuagint twice reads a third-person masculine plural pronoun (αὐτούς and αὐτοῖς) where the word in the Masoretic Text is להן; cf. Brooke and McLean, *Old Testament in Greek*, 888. The word in the Masoretic Text is not taken to be a pronoun, but rather a conjunction meaning "therefore"; cf. BDB, 530.

27. BDB, 773.

28. Hubbard, *Ruth*, 122 n. 14. He observes that the two words sound alike and that the verb shares two of the name's consonants except in reverse order.

This difference is significant for exegesis in that it allows a more nuanced understanding of the passage.[29]

Ruth 2:1

There is a Kethiv-Qere variant in 2:1, with more than twenty medieval manuscripts agreeing with the Qere.[30] The two text forms are as follows:

Kethiv	מְיֻדָּע
Qere	מוֹדַע

The Kethiv is a pual participle from the root יד״ע, usually rendered "acquaintance."[31] The Qere is a noun from the same root, usually translated "kinsman."[32] (A noun form closely related to the Qere is used later in the book at 3:2.) It is evident that one form is primary and the other secondary. The letters ו and ׳ are susceptible to accidental confusion, but perhaps there is an intentional change here. The Qere may be the result of adapting the text of 2:1 to the related noun used in 3:2. This difference does have some bearing on exegesis. If the Kethiv is original, the author used a general form to refer to Boaz in chapter 2, and then used a specific term to refer to him in chapter 3.[33] If this was the case, it would serve to heighten the sense of climax with the more specific mention in chapter 3. Reading with the Kethiv does express a nuance that otherwise, if the Qere were original, would not be in evidence.

Ruth 2:6

The Syriac omits words that correspond to the Masoretic Text's הַנִּצָּב עַל־הַקּוֹצְרִים in 2:6. The student may assume that

29. Campbell, *Ruth*, 77, supports the originality of the Masoretic Text against the Greek and Old Latin.
30. Hubbard, *Ruth*, 132, indicates that the Vulgate also agrees with the Qere.
31. BDB, 394.
32. Ibid., 396.
33. Hubbard, *Ruth*, 132–33, rightly points out that the Qere would be redundant in 2:1, since it states that Boaz was a part of the clan of Elimelech.

the versions support the Masoretic Text unless otherwise indicated by *BHS*. In this case, a check of the Cambridge Septuagint shows that the Septuagint has Greek words that correspond to the Masoretic Text.[34] These words are admittedly redundant (cf. v. 5), but the agreement of the Masoretic Text and the Septuagint against Syriac suggests that the words are original and were probably dropped by the Syriac as a simplification in the translation process.

Ruth 2:7

The first textual difficulty mentioned in the *BHS* apparatus for 2:7 (marked with the letter *a*) is rather minor: the Septuagint reads ἀπὸ πρωίθεν καὶ ἕως ἑσπέρας where the Masoretic Text reads מֵאָז הַבֹּקֶר וְעַד־עַתָּה.[35] The equivalence מֵאָז = ἀπό, not mentioned in the *BHS* apparatus, merits a study of its own, but for the present this must be bypassed. In reference to the *BHS* note, this is the only place in the Septuagint where עַתָּה is rendered by the word ἑσπέρας ("evening"). The Hebrew word most usually translated by this Greek word is some form of עֶרֶב.[36] With these details in mind, a plausible explanation may be suggested. The Septuagint translator may have paraphrased the text. The word עַתָּה ("now") in context appears to refer to a time late in the day, and the translator may have simply expressed one understanding of the sense of the text with the word ἑσπέρας. This suggested solution takes it that the listing of Hatch and Redpath in this case does not indicate any kind of direct semantic equivalence between the Hebrew and Greek word pair.

The second, and major, textual difficulty of 2:7 (marked with the repeated letters *b–b*) is especially important—since

---

34. Brooke and McLean, *Old Testament in Greek*, 890.

35. It should be noted that the testimony of Septuagint for עַתָּה = ἑσπέρας is not unanimous. The textual note in Brooke and McLean, *Old Testament in Greek*, 890, indicates that five cursives (one is a corrector), the Armenian version, a corrector of the Ethiopic version, and the Old Latin all reflect the Masoretic Text, עַתָּה = νῦν. This reading may be the result of a revision to agree with the Masoretic Text, but it still should be noted in a study of the text.

36. Edwin Hatch and Henry A. Redpath, *Concordance to the Septuagint* (Oxford: Clarendon, 1897; repr. Grand Rapids: Baker, 1987), 1:557.

the Masoretic Text is admittedly difficult.[37] The variants given in *BHS* are as follows:

MT   זֶה שִׁבְתָּהּ הַבַּיִת

LXX   οὐ κατέπαυσεν ἐν τῷ ἀγρῷ

Robinson suggests that the Septuagint corresponds to an original Hebrew that read לֹא שָׁבְתָה בַשָּׂדֶה. Since the Masoretic Text is difficult, we begin with the translation of the Septuagint: "She did not rest in the field." The supposed Hebrew original suggested in *BHS* means exactly the same as the Septuagint. Yet it is not easy to visualize how the Masoretic Text could have resulted from the presumed original Hebrew that stands behind the Septuagint. It is true that the middle word, in terms of its consonants, is identical. But it is very difficult to imagine how לֹא could have become corrupted into זֶה, and it is even more difficult to see how בַשָּׂדֶה could have been changed into הַבַּיִת. We are not dealing with just the interchange of a pair of letters here, but with an interchange of a total of six pairs of letters in two words. It would be next to impossible to demonstrate a plausible pathway for such changes. Moreover, of the six pairs, only one (ה and ת) is attested as a likely interchange.[38] It must be admitted that there is no suitable mechanism for the necessary development from the supposed *Vorlage* of the Septuagint reading into the reading now attested in the Masoretic Text.

Is it possible, then, to make any sense out of the current Masoretic Text? The last phrase of 2:7 yields, as a literal translation, "This [masc.] her sitting/dwelling the house (a) little."[39] Hubbard, noting that זֶה is a masculine pronoun, takes its antecedent as "field" in 2:3 and offers the following translation: "This field has been her residence; the house (in town)

37. As the Cambridge Septuagint shows, the situation is more complex than indicated in the *BHS* apparatus. The treatment here, however, will concentrate on the problem listed in *BHS*. Hubbard, *Ruth*, 2, describes this textual problem as the only "unsolvable" difficulty in the book.

38. See chapter 6 for details.

39. This is the translation offered in Hubbard, *Ruth*, 150–52, which work should be consulted for its thorough treatment of this difficult verse.

has meant little to her."[40] The text is admittedly difficult, and perhaps there cannot be certainty in the translation. From what has been said above, however, it does not appear that the rendering of the Septuagint is of any help in restoring a more pristine state of the Hebrew text. It would appear that the Hebrew text was as difficult for the Septuagint translator as it is for the modern reader. The Septuagint read the middle word of the Hebrew text with a different vocalization, and offers an interpretative translation for the rest of the verse that has the effect of making Ruth's energetic work and persistence even greater. According to the Septuagint, she did not rest at all during her day of gleaning![41]

Ruth 2:16

The single letter *a* preceding the first word of 2:16, which is not paired with another *a* in the verse, indicates that the note refers to the entire verse. The note indicates that the Syriac omits the verse. There is some sense of repetition in 2:16 of the ideas of 2:15, and perhaps a scribe or translator deleted it as unnecessary. The verse is in the Septuagint, though in an expanded form,[42] and there is no chance for its loss through haplography or its inclusion in the Masoretic Text by way of dittography. It should be accepted as the preferred reading.

Ruth 2:18

The note indicated by the letter *a* contains the following readings:

MT   וַתֵּרֶא

40. Ibid., 151. Hubbard holds that Ruth had waited for Boaz to arrive at the field, instead of the traditional understanding that she had worked all day in the field. He suggests that the enigmatic phrase at the end of 2:7 may reflect the servant's confused state of mind or an otherwise unknown idiom or custom.

41. For other suggested solutions to this textual problem, see Campbell, *Ruth*, 94–96; and Barthélemy, *Critique Textuelle*, 131–32. The point needs to be emphasized that this is the only place in the text of Ruth where we are unable to determine a solution and thus have a firm basis for exegesis.

42. Cf. Hubbard, *Ruth*, 171 n. 6.

a few medieval Hebrew   וַתֵּרֶא[43]
manuscripts, Syriac, Vulgate

The Masoretic Text translates, "And her mother-in-law saw
what she had gleaned." The reading of the medieval manuscripts, Syriac, and Vulgate translates, "And she [Ruth]
showed her mother-in-law what she had gleaned." The Masoretic Text has a qal verb, and the medieval manuscripts a
hiphil of the same root. There is obviously a difference in detail here. Barthélemy argues that the absence of a second accusative particle (אֵת) before "her mother-in-law" supports
the Masoretic Text,[44] but the lack of אֵת with the first of two ac-
cusatives, especially the person, is acceptable Hebrew syntax.[45] The flow of the text is better with the reading of the
(three to ten) medieval manuscripts and the two versions
(Ruth is the consistent subject of all verbs in the verse). This
would mean that the Masoretic Text (along with the Septuagint) is more difficult, and therefore some would argue that
the reading of the Masoretic Text is original.[46]

Ruth 2:19

The repeated letters *a–a* in 2:19 bracket four words of the
Hebrew text. The variants are as follows:

MT   אֵת אֲשֶׁר־עָשְׂתָה עִמּוֹ

LXX   ποῦ ἐποίησεν

The Masoretic Text translates, "With whom she had worked";
the Septuagint yields, "Where she had worked." In most of this
verse there is an exact correspondence between the words of
the Hebrew and the words of the Septuagint. The only difference between the two texts, other than the variant mentioned

43. Barthélemy, *Critique Textuelle*, 133, indicates that only two medieval
manuscripts have this reading and that they are of doubtful authority.
44. Ibid.
45. Waltke and O'Connor, *Biblical Hebrew Syntax*, 441–42.
46. Barthélemy, *Critique Textuelle*, 133. See also the translations of the
New International Version, New American Standard Bible, and Jerusalem Bible.

in the apparatus, is that where the Masoretic Text has "she told her mother-in-law" the Septuagint has "Ruth told her mother-in-law." That the rest of the verse is so literally translated argues for a Hebrew *Vorlage* for the Septuagint of this verse that was different from the text now found in the Masoretic Text. The question then is which of these two Hebrew texts is more likely primary. Two considerations argue that the Masoretic Text represents the original. First of all, the use of the proper name Ruth in the Septuagint of this verse instead of the simple "she told" of the Masoretic Text appears to be a sign of a more popular text. Second, the reading of the Septuagint in Ruth's answer to Naomi's question corresponds exactly to a part of the question. It is probable that the slightly different form of Ruth's response was original and was adjusted by a scribe to the precise form of Naomi's question. Whether it was done purposefully or unintentionally cannot be determined.

Ruth 2:20

A single note for 2:20 in the apparatus, marked by the letter *a*, indicates the following variants:

MT	לַיהוָה[47]
a single medieval manuscript and the Syriac	omit לְ[48]

The Masoretic Text yields the translation, "May he [Boaz] be blessed by Yahweh." The omission of לְ changes the meaning significantly, for it gives the translation, "May Yahweh be blessed."[49] Which of the two readings is likely original? Two points indicate that the Masoretic Text, with the agreement of the Septuagint, is primary. A single medieval manuscript, the

47. The form of the tetragrammaton is a *Qere perpetuum*. See the explanation in chapter 2.

48. Campbell, *Ruth*, 88, adds that the Old Latin also supports this reading, information that is not given in *BHS*.

49. Perhaps a more literal translation of בָּרוּךְ הוּא יְהוָה would be "may he be blessed, that is, Yahweh." This formula does not appear elsewhere in the Masoretic Text, but an analogous expression is found in Isa. 19:25: בָּרוּךְ עַמִּי מִצְרַיִם ("may my people be blessed, that is, Egypt"). The usual formula for "may Yahweh be blessed" is simply בָּרוּךְ יְהוָה (without the pronoun הוּא); cf. Gen. 9:26.

Syriac, and the Old Latin are not strong enough evidence to overturn the evidence of the Masoretic Text and the Septuagint. In addition, the familiarity of the phrase *may Yahweh be blessed* argues that the direction of the change would be from the Masoretic Text to that of the medieval manuscript, not the reverse. So while the variant in this verse does affect exegesis, there is good evidence to follow the Masoretic Text.

Ruth 2:21

A single note for 2:21 is indicated by the letter *a*. The variants are as follows:

MT	הַמּוֹאֲבִיָּה
LXX, Syriac, Vulgate	omit הַמּוֹאֲבִיָּה (LXX and Syriac [generally] add πρὸς τὴν πενθερὰν αὐτῆς in its place)

Ruth is referred to in various places in the book as a "Moabitess." It could be argued that the word was inadvertently added in 2:21 at some time by a Jewish scribe, but it could also have been dropped from the *Vorlage* of the versions or by the translators/revisers themselves. As to the addition in the Septuagint and Syriac, it is obvious in the context that Ruth is speaking to her mother-in-law and, as Hubbard points out, this addition in the Septuagint is as redundant as the Masoretic Text. He also indicates that the use of "Moabitess" may serve as an "inclusio of identity" since it introduces Ruth's first and last words in the chapter.[50] Thus we probably have another example of the Septuagint making the implicit explicit. The Masoretic Text should be retained.

Ruth 2:23

The note for 2:23 is marked with the letters *a–a*.[51] The variants are as follows:

50. Hubbard, *Ruth*, 182 n. 7.
51. Campbell, *Ruth*, 88, lists a possible variant for this verse that is not registered in *BHS*. The Masoretic Text reads qal infinitive כְּלֹת, but the Septuagint suggests a possible piel infinitive כַּלֹּת. The Lucianic recension uses an indicative, "They completed."

MT   וַתֵּשֶׁב אֶת

a few medieval Hebrew manu-   וַתָּשָׁב אֶל
scripts and the Vulgate

The Masoretic Text yields the translation, "She lived with her mother-in-law." Three to ten medieval manuscripts and the Vulgate read a different set of vowels for the verb and a different preposition: "She returned to her mother-in-law." The letters ת and ל are not easily confused. The Masoretic Text, supported by the Septuagint, is probably original, although there is no great difference in meaning, in context, between the two readings. The Masoretic Text and the Septuagint refer to a state, Ruth's living with her mother-in-law for a period of time. The medieval manuscripts and the Vulgate refer to an event that occurred at the end of the activities described in chapter 2.

Ruth 3:3

The first of two notes in 3:3 is marked by the letter *a*. The variants are as follows:

Kethiv   שִׂמְלֹתֵךְ

Qere   שִׂמְלֹתַיִךְ[52]

The Kethiv (and more than twenty medieval manuscripts) refers to "your garment [singular]," while the Qere (and a few medieval manuscripts) refers to "your garments [plural]." The usage of the singular and plural forms of this noun is just about even in the Old Testament.[53] Hubbard reads the Kethiv, but takes the singular as a collective.[54] Perhaps the Qere was

52. Campbell, *Ruth*, 120, gives information for the versions that is not listed in *BHS*. The Septuagint reads the singular, in agreement with the Kethiv, while the Syriac, Vulgate, and Targum read the plural, in agreement with the Qere.

53. Solomon Mandelkern, *Veteris Testamenti Concordantiae* (Tel Aviv: Schocken, 1971), 1126, shows fifteen uses of the singular and thirteen uses of the plural. Among these, Ruth 3:3 and 2 Sam. 12:20 reflect a Kethiv-Qere variant. In both cases the Kethiv is singular and the Qere plural.

54. Hubbard, *Ruth*, 197 n. 7.

motivated by the idea that if Ruth was wearing only one garment, she would have had to use that garment to carry the gift of Boaz's grain home with her. Sasson argues that Ruth wore two garments: the שִׂמְלָה of 3:3 (the main garment) and the מִטְפַּחַת of 3:15 (a supplementary garment, used either as a veil or to ward off the coolness of the night air).[55]

The second textual note in 3:3 is also a Kethiv-Qere, and is marked by the letter *b*. The variants are as follows:

Kethiv	וְיָרַדְתִּי
Qere	וְיָרַדְתְּ

In this case, more than twenty medieval manuscripts agree with the Qere. Apparently the Kethiv is an archaic form of the qal perfect second-person feminine singular verb.[56] The direction of the change is very likely from the archaic Kethiv to the normal Qere instead of the reverse. The basic issue is grammatical custom.

Ruth 3:4

A Kethiv-Qere in 3:4 is marked by the letter *a*. The readings are as follows:

Kethiv	וְשָׁכָבְתִּי
Qere	וְשָׁכָבְתְּ

Presumably, although there is no explicit indication in the note in *BHS*, a number of medieval manuscripts read with the Qere as in the previous case. The explanation of this Kethiv-Qere is exactly the same as for note *b* in 3:3.

Ruth 3:5

A special category of Kethiv-Qere variant in 3:5 is marked by the letter *a*. The observant reader will notice that the next to last word of the verse consists of only the vowels for the

55. Sasson, *Ruth*, 68.
56. See GKC §44h; Hubbard, *Ruth*, 197 n. 8; and Campbell, *Ruth*, 120.

word אֱלַי, printed without the consonants אלי above them. In this case more than twenty medieval manuscripts read with the Qere, but the Septuagint reads with the Kethiv, omitting the preposition and suffix.

Würthwein classifies this situation as an example of *itture sopherim*, but both Yeivin and Ginsburg list it as a separate category.[57] The reader should note that the Masorah parva in the margin gives data that agrees with the numbers of Yeivin: "אלי: one of ten times [that a word is] read but not written." While this case is interesting from the point of view of the transmission of the text, it has little effect on exegesis. The thought of אֱלַי is clearly implicit in the context, and perhaps for that reason we should argue that the omission of the word is original. In both English and Hebrew one may equally say, "What you say I will do," or, "What you say to me I will do." If anything, the former (in English, at least) is more idiomatic in speech. The latter is more formal. If this is the way things happened, it indicates that the Masoretes themselves sometimes made the implicit explicit.

Ruth 3:6

The variants are as follows for the note in 3:6 marked with the letter *a*:

MT	כְּכֹל
a few medieval manuscripts, Syriac, Vulgate	כֹל

In this case, although not noted in the apparatus, the Septuagint agrees with the Masoretic Text. Assuming that the Mas-

---

57. Ernst Würthwein, *The Text of the Old Testament*, trans. Erroll F. Rhodes (Grand Rapids: Eerdmans, 1979), 19. Israel Yeivin, *Introduction to the Tiberian Masorah*, trans. and ed. E. John Revell (Missoula, Mont.: Scholars Press, 1980), 51, limits the *itture sopherim* to the five places in the Hebrew Bible where a *wāw* is expected but not used (e.g., Gen. 18:5). On page 58 he mentions that the Masorah lists ten places where a word is to be read even though it is not written. Würthwein mentions only seven such passages. Cf. also Christian D. Ginsburg, *Introduction to the Massoretico-Critical Edition of the Hebrew Bible* (London: Trinitarian Bible Society, 1897; reprinted with prolegomenon by Harry M. Orlinsky: New York: Ktav, 1966), 308–9.

oretic Text is original, the reading of the medieval manuscripts, Syriac, and Vulgate could have resulted from haplography (a scribe would have copied only one כ instead of two). On the other hand, if the reading of (three to ten) medieval manuscripts is primary, the Masoretic Text could have resulted from dittography (a scribe may have written two כs instead of the single one in the exemplar). Here we see that two widely evidenced accidental changes can explain the change in the text in two opposite ways. The Masoretic Text, as it stands, is an example of *kap veritatis* and should be translated "exactly as."[58]

Ruth 3:7

The letter *a* in 3:7 refers to the omission of a verb וַיֵּשְׁתְּ in the Septuagint.[59] Perhaps the translators left this verb out in order to downplay the possibility of any kind of impropriety in this meeting between Ruth and Boaz. It is also possible that the verb was not original in this verse, but was added under the influence (conscious or accidental) of Naomi's words in 3:3. The conscious omission by the translators in this case is perhaps more likely, given the general character of their tendencies.

Ruth 3:9

The first of three notes to 3:9 is marked by the letter *a*. The Lucianic recension of the Septuagint, in general agreement with the Syriac and Vulgate, adds αὐτῇ to this verse, and Robinson suggests that this corresponded to לָהּ in the Hebrew text from which Lucian worked. This is probably a change in the direction of expected usage. The Masoretic Text, with the agreement of the rest of the Septuagint, is probably original and may well serve to emphasize Boaz's state of shock when he awoke with a start and discovered a girl sleeping at his feet.

---

58. See Waltke and O'Connor, *Biblical Hebrew Syntax*, 202–3.

59. Hubbard, *Ruth*, 206 n. 1, mentions that the Septuagint and Syriac "inexplicably" omit the verb *and drank*.

The note marked with the letter *b* indicates an idiosyncrasy of the Leningrad Codex, which served as the basis for the text of *BHS*. The person responsible for the pointing of the Leningrad Codex made an obvious error in omitting *shewa* under ה, a scribal error that can be corrected by comparing other early Hebrew manuscripts and editions.

The variant marked with the letter *c* refers to a special kind of Kethiv-Qere: the Kethiv is split into two readings: western or Tiberian (indicated by K^{Occ}) and eastern or Babylonian (K^{Or}, which is also in agreement with the Qere). The variants are as follows:

Kethiv^{Occ}	כְּנָפֶיךָ
Kethiv^{Or}, Qere, LXX, Syriac	כְּנָפֶךָ[60]

The western Kethiv and more than twenty medieval manuscripts read "your wings," while the eastern Kethiv, Qere, Septuagint, and Syriac read "your wing." Hubbard, mentioning that most commentators read the singular, translates "your garment-corner."[61] The idiom here is explained by a similar reference in Ezekiel 16:8, where a singular form for "to spread the corner of a garment over a woman" is used in reference to entering into a marriage relationship. Thus interpreted, Ruth is proposing marriage to Boaz with her words.[62]

Ruth 3:11

Note *a* for 3:11 indicates that a few (three to ten) medieval manuscripts, Origen's fifth column, the Syriac, the Targum, and the Vulgate all add אֵלַי or its equivalent at this point. This

---

60. The Septuagint reads τὸ πτερύγιόν σου; cf. Brooke and McLean, *Old Testament in Greek*, 893.

61. Hubbard, *Ruth*, 207.

62. There is an interesting word association that should not be missed in the use of this word in Ruth 3:9, albeit in the singular. In Ruth 2:12 the plural form was used to speak of Ruth's finding protection under Yahweh's wings. Here in 3:9 she is asking for protection by becoming married to Boaz. Perhaps the western Kethiv and the medieval readings resulted from assimilation to the form of 2:12.

is very likely a change that makes the implicit explicit (see similar changes at 3:5a, 9a).

Ruth 3:12

The note marked *a* in 3:12 presents another kind of specialized Kethiv-Qere, this time the opposite of that in 3:5. The Kethiv contains אם; the Qere, in agreement with more than twenty medieval manuscripts, reads nothing at this point. The Kethiv-Qere in 3:5 was "read, not written." Here in verse 12 it is "written, not read." The note in the Masorah parva reads "אם: one of eight times that a word is written but not read."[63] Hubbard suggests that אם here is an error and explains its presence as a dittography from אם in 3:13 or אמרם in 3:12.[64] It is also possible, however, to read the Kethiv and make good sense of the text. In that case the translation would be, "And now, it is indeed true. (I can say nothing) except that I am your kinsmen."[65] There is a difference here that depends on whether אם is read, but the overall effect on exegesis is minor.

Ruth 3:14

We now come to the verse in Ruth with the most notes in *BHS*. The first note is indicated by the letter *a* and concerns a Kethiv-Qere. The Kethiv may be pointed מַרְגְּלֹתָו or מַרְגְּלֹתוֹ. The first is a plural spelled defectively; the second is a singular. The Qere (also the reading of more than twenty medieval

63. Würthwein, *Text of the Old Testament*, 19, lists five passages where this phenomenon is found. Yeivin, *Tiberian Masorah*, 58, agrees with the Masorah parva in speaking of eight occurrences.

64. If it is dittography, it is more than simple dittography. If its presence is due to 3:13, it could hardly be classed as dittography. It is more a case of a stray אם being introduced into 3:12. Presumably the scribe's eye slipped to אם in 3:13 and then back to the very place it left in 3:12. That in *BHS* the two words are one above the other indicates nothing about their position in the early scrolls. If אם in 3:12 is derived from אמרם, it again is not simple dittography. If א and ם correspond to their partners in אמרם, then something also happened to ב and ו in the middle of the word.

65. This translation is based on understanding the first כי as an emphatic particle; cf. BDB, 472. The ellipsis preceding כי אם is suggested by GKC §163d.

manuscripts) has מַרְגְּלֹתָיו. Elsewhere in the Old Testament, this noun exists only as a plural, which suggests that the only difference between the Kethiv and the Qere is that the Kethiv is spelled defectively and the Qere is spelled plene. If the Kethiv is to be pointed as a singular, it is without parallel in the Old Testament.

The note indicated by the letter *b* gives another Kethiv-Qere. If the Kethiv (בְּמָרֹם) is correct, it is the only time that the word is spelled this way in the Old Testament. The word is obviously used in the same way as טֶרֶם is used in other contexts, so the word is either a variant spelling or a simple error with the extraneous ו.[66]

The note introduced by the letter *c* is a bit more complicated. The Septuagint (the Vulgate generally agrees) adds βοος (Boaz) after the verb. This is probably another example of the Septuagint making the implicit explicit. The Syriac, on the other hand, reads the equivalent of וַתֹּאמֶר ("she said") instead of the Masoretic Text's וַיֹּאמֶר ("he said"). The Syriac reading is related to the following two notes.

The note marked with the letter *d* indicates that the Syriac reads the equivalent of בָּאתִי instead of the Masoretic Text's בָאָה.

The final note indicated for 3:14, marked with the letter *e*, indicates that הָאִשָּׁה is not found in the Syriac, and that the Septuagint reads γυνή, possibly reflecting a Hebrew original without the definite article (אִשָּׁה). So the total effect of these changes in the Syriac leads to the following translation: "And she said, 'Do not let it be known that I came to the threshing floor.' " The rendering of the Syriac is thus drastically different from the Masoretic Text (or even from the Septuagint). Hubbard argues for the originality of the Masoretic Text and understands the use of the verb אָמַר as referring to internal speech:[67] "He said to himself, 'Let it not be known that the woman came to the threshing floor.' " It appears that the Syriac is an interpretative change and that the Masoretic Text is arguably original.

66. BDB, 382; and Hubbard, *Ruth*, 220 n. 2.
67. Hubbard, *Ruth*, 220 n. 3.

Ruth 3:15

The first of two notes to 3:15 is marked with the letter *a*. After וַיֹּאמֶר ("he said") of the Masoretic Text, the Septuagint adds αὐτῇ and Lucian's recension of the Septuagint alters this to τῇ Ρουθ. Both changes reflect the tendency of the Septuagint to make the implicit explicit. Even if the Septuagint or Lucian reflect a possible different Hebrew original, the difference would not be greatly significant for exegesis.

The second note is marked by the letter *b*. The variants are as follows:

MT	וַיָּבֹא
Syriac, Vulgate, many medieval manuscripts	וַתָּבֹא[68]

The Masoretic Text yields a translation, "He [Boaz] went to the city." The medieval manuscripts (more than twenty) plus the cited versions translate as, "She [Ruth] went to the city."[69] Hubbard follows the Masoretic Text and translates the idiom as "He entered the city." He argues that a reference to Ruth here in verse 15 would make the first verb in 3:16 redundant.[70]

Ruth 3:17

The note marked with the letter *a* indicates that the Septuagint adds αὐτῇ after וַתֹּאמֶר. The note further refers the reader

68. Barthélemy, *Critique Textuelle*, 133, points out that Greek verbs in third-person do not specify gender and this makes the reading in Greek ambiguous. Additionally he points out that some Greek manuscripts (l, o, e₂) read Ruth as the explicit subject of the verb in question, but that at least one manuscript (w) reads Boaz as the explicit subject of the verb.

69. This particular textual variant has had an interesting role in the history of the Authorized Version, the first two editions of which differed, among other things, in their rendering of this verse. One followed the Masoretic Text and was called the "He Bible," while the other followed the Vulgate and was called the "She Bible." Cf. Allen Wikgren, "The English Bible," in *The Interpreter's Bible*, ed. George A. Buttrick (New York: Abingdon, 1952), 1:94.

70. Hubbard, *Ruth*, 220 n. 10. Cf. also the argument in Louise P. Smith, "The Book of Ruth: Introduction and Exegesis," in *The Interpreter's Bible*, ed. George A. Buttrick (New York: Abingdon, 1953), 2:847; and Barthélemy, *Critique Textuelle*, 133.

to 3:15 note *a*, where a similar occurrence was cited, and, as there, the characteristic of making the implicit explicit is probably the explanation.

The second note for 3:17 is marked with a letter *b*. The details of the note are identical with the discussion of the variant dealt with under 3:5 note *a*.

Ruth 4:2

The note marked with the letter *a* indicates that the Septuagint and the Vulgate add the name βοος (Boaz) as the subject of the verb וַיִּקַּח. There is a slight possibility of ambiguity in the wording of the Masoretic Text, since the last two verbs of 4:1 refer to the nearer kinsman. But the context of the entire passage makes clear that Boaz is in fact the subject of the first verb in 4:2, and therefore the change in the Septuagint and Vulgate is simply making the implicit explicit.[71]

Ruth 4:3

The note marked with the letters *a–a* refers to two words in the Masoretic Text: מָכְרָה נָעֳמִי. The Septuagint reading for these two words is ἣ δέδοται Νωεμειν. The Masoretic Text yields this translation: "Naomi is going to sell the part of the field that belonged to our relative Elimelech."[72] The text of the Septuagint yields, "The part of the field that belongs to our relative Elimelech, that was given to Naomi." It will be noted that the Septuagint reading is not a complete sentence and that the Masoretic Text makes good sense as it stands. Hubbard argues that the rendering of the Septuagint is probably an erroneous interpretation of the Masoretic Text and should not be considered as a translation of the Masoretic Text.[73] It is best, therefore, to prefer the Masoretic Text.

71. Cf. Hubbard, *Ruth*, 232 n. 3, who suggests that "clarity requires that the translation identify the subject" of this verb. It may be argued that the Masoretic Text is clear when viewed in context.

72. Ibid., 239, where Hubbard discusses the translation of this perfect verb.

73. Ibid., 236 n. 4.

Ruth 4:4

The first of two notes for 4:4 is marked by the letter *a*. The variants are as follows:

MT	יִגְאַל
many medieval manuscripts, most versions	תִּגְאַל

The reading of the more than twenty medieval manuscripts and the versions is probably the easier reading. It agrees with the expected flow of the passage and corresponds to the preceding verb form, אִם־תִּגְאַל, where Boaz spoke to the nearer kinsman and said, "If you will redeem."[74] The Masoretic Text is clearly the more difficult reading, yet it may be too difficult. Hubbard characterizes it as "overly abrupt."[75] In this case, the versions may reflect the original reading. If so, the cause of the Masoretic Text's reading is best classed as an accidental change.[76] Is it possible, however, to understand the Masoretic Text in a way that makes sense? Sasson suggests that the phrase in question was spoken, almost parenthetically, to the elders before whom this transaction was being conducted.[77] Such an understanding yields the following translation: "If you will redeem, then redeem—[an aside to the elders:] and if he will not redeem—[again speaking directly to the nearer kinsman:] tell me." Certainty is probably not attainable in this case. It is possible to make sense out of both the Masoretic Text and the versions. The critic may decide to accept the more difficult reading (the Masoretic Text) or to judge the Masoretic Text as "too difficult." In this case the reading of the medieval manuscripts and the versions will be judged original.

The second note for 4:4, marked by the letter *b*, concerns another Kethiv-Qere:

74. Ibid., 237 n. 5, where the translation "act as kinsman-redeemer" is defended.
75. Ibid., 237 n. 6.
76. There is no easily explained mechanism for the confusion of ה and י. See chapter 6.
77. Sasson, *Ruth*, 118.

Kethiv	וְאֵדַע
Qere, many medieval manuscripts	וְאֵדְעָה

The Kethiv is a qal imperfect plus a simple *wāw*, and the Qere is the corresponding qal cohortative plus a simple *wāw*. The same translation fits both: "Tell me so that I will know."[78]

Ruth 4:5

There are two notes for 4:5, and the two are interrelated. The note marked with the letter *a* indicates that the Vulgate reads *quoque*, and Robinson suggests that the Masoretic Text (וּמֵאֵת),[79] supported by the Septuagint, should be emended to גַּם אֶת־ on that basis. The major problem with the Masoretic Text as it stands is that the second use of the verb קָנָה has no direct object.[80] For this reason a strong consensus emends the text, with the backing of the versions, to וְגַם אֶת־רוּת.[81]

Much could be written about the problems of 4:5. But it must be remembered that the main aim of this chapter is the examination of the textual data of the Book of Ruth and not the complete solution of each difficulty. Thus the second textual note, marked with the letter *b*, needs to be mentioned. The note indicates the presence of yet another Kethiv-Qere. The data are as follows:

Kethiv	קָנִיתִי
Qere	קָנִיתָה

78. See Waltke and O'Connor, *Biblical Hebrew Syntax*, 650 / §39.2.2a; 575 / §34.5.2b.

79. Brooke and McLean, *Old Testament in Greek*, 895, reads καὶ παρὰ Ῥούθ as the equivalent of the Masoretic Text's וּמֵאֵת. Actually the Septuagint reading represents something of a conflate for it yields a translation as follows: "When you buy the field from Naomi and from Ruth . . . , you also must acquire her [Ruth] so that you may raise up the name of the dead one over his inheritance." The Septuagint thus represents in its rendering both the reading of the Masoretic Text and Robinson's suggested reading in *BHS*.

80. Hubbard, *Ruth*, 237 n. 8, calls this a "grammatically awkward situation."

81. Ibid. Cf. also Sasson, *Ruth*, 122.

The Kethiv is a qal perfect first-person common singular verb, "I acquired," while the Qere is the corresponding second-person masculine singular form, "You acquired (or acquire)." The Kethiv here seems to make little sense, although it has been defended by both Beattie and Sasson.[82] Robinson suggests that the Hebrew text should be emended to קְנֵה on the basis of the versions. Two comments are in order. In my opinion this is one of the cases where the difficult reading is too difficult, and it should not be retained. The Qere should be taken as the best reading in conjunction with the majority of modern commentators.[83] As to the suggestion of emending to the qal imperative, it appears that the Septuagint, at least, has translated the sense of the passage rather than an explicit imperative form. Except for three words, the Septuagint is a rather literal translation.

Ruth 4:6

There is no note in the apparatus of *BHS* for 4:6, but the Masorah parva mentions a Kethiv-Qere. The Kethiv is לִגְאוֹל, and the Qere is the more normal לִגְאָל־. The note in the Masorah parva continues: "This is a superfluous *wāw*; it is one of two times that it is written plene in the language."[84] The reason that the *wāw* is superfluous is that the word is joined to the following word with *maqqep*, and therefore the vowel should be short. This is simply a spelling variation.

Ruth 4:7

The first of two notes for 4:7 is marked with the letter *a*. The Septuagint, with agreement from the Syriac, Targum,

---

82. D. R. G. Beattie, "Kethibh and Qere in Ruth iv 5," *Vetus Testamentum* 21 (1971): 490–94; Sasson, *Ruth*, 122–31.

83. Hubbard, *Ruth*, 237. Even though a fully defended solution for this verse cannot be given within the limits of this chapter, the following is a suggested translation that follows the Masoretic Text in regard to note *a* and reads with the Qere in regard to note *b*: "Boaz said, 'When you acquire the field from Naomi, you acquire [it] from Ruth the Moabitess, the wife of the dead man, in order to raise up the name of the dead man over his inheritance.'" If the emendation for note *a* is accepted, Boaz would be saying, "You must also acquire Ruth the Moabitess . . . to raise up the name. . . ."

84. The infinitive construct of this root was also spelled plene in 4:4.

and Vulgate, adds τὸ δικαίωμα. The Masoretic Text reads
וְזֹאת לְפָנִים בְּיִשְׂרָאֵל: "Now this was previously [what happened]
in Israel with regard to redemption and exchange [of prop-
erty]." The Septuagint renders the phrase in a more explicit
sense, "This was formerly the regulation in regard to redemption and exchange [of property]." There seems to be no
easily explained reason for the loss of הַמִּשְׁפָּט from the Masoretic Text, so this is probably another example of an addition
in the Septuagint (and other versions) that serves to make an
implicit feature of the Masoretic Text explicit in the Greek
translation. This use of וְזֹאת, where the reference is to an action or circumstance that is vaguely defined, is called a *neu-
trum* pronoun.[85]

The second note in 4:7 is marked by the letter *b*. The Septuagint and the Targum place a copula before the verb שָׁלַף.
The presence of the *wāw* is probably the more normal grammar, whereas the asyndetic expression is more unusual. The
Masoretic Text should probably be retained.

Ruth 4:8

The wording of the Masoretic Text in 4:8 is somewhat
terse: "And the kinsman said to Boaz, 'Acquire it for yourself,'
and he took off his shoe." The Septuagint expands this by adding the phrase καὶ ἔδωκεν αὐτῷ after the last word of the Masoretic Text. In context, this action of the nearer kinsman is
obviously implied in the Masoretic Text of 4:7. The most reasonable explanation is that the Septuagint has again made the
implicit explicit.

Ruth 4:10

The note in 4:10 is marked by the repeated letters *a–a*. The
variants are as follows:

MT   וּמִשַּׁעַר מְקוֹמוֹ

LXX   καὶ ἐκ τῆς φυλῆς λαοῦ αὐτοῦ

85. Waltke and O'Connor, *Biblical Hebrew Syntax*, 312 / §17.4.3b.

The Masoretic Text translates "and from the gate of his place," while the Septuagint translates "and from the tribe of his people." Robinson suggests that the Septuagint represents a variant Hebrew reading of מֵעַמּוֹ. A better suggestion is that the Septuagint translator may have read וּמִשְׁפַּחַת עַמּוֹ ("and from the family or clan of his people"). Another suggestion is that the Septuagint represents an interpretive translation of the Masoretic Text. Note the one-to-one correspondence between the number of morphemes in the two readings above and in the literal translations of each. If there was a variant reading in the *Vorlage* of the Septuagint that read וּמִשְׁפַּחַת עַמּוֹ or מֵעַמּוֹ, perhaps it was the replacement of a less typical reading (the Masoretic Text) with a more typical reading.

Ruth 4:11

A single note in the apparatus for 4:11 is marked by the letters *a–a*. The variants follow:

MT	וְהַזְּקֵנִים עֵדִים
LXX	Μάρτυρες. καὶ οἱ πρεσβύτεροι εἴποσαν

Robinson suggests that the Septuagint reflects a Hebrew text that read עֵדִים וַיֹּאמְרוּ הַזְּקֵנִים. If this Hebrew text was original, then three changes must have taken place. The word וַיֹּאמְרוּ must have fallen out of the text; the words הַזְּקֵנִים and עֵדִים must have been transposed; and *wāw* must have been added to הַזְּקֵנִים. There is no easily explained mechanism for these changes. In addition, in the preceding examination of the text of Ruth it has been noted that the Septuagint has taken noticeable liberties with the text in several places. The Masoretic Text is the shorter reading and, for that reason, is probably the primary reading. The Septuagint may depend on a variant Hebrew text or the changes may have come about in the translation (or revision) process. The Masoretic Text, as it stands, may be translated: "And all the people who were in the gate [the onlookers] and the elders said, 'We are witnesses.' "[86]

---

86. Cf. the discussion in Hubbard, *Ruth*, 253 n. 9, who also retains the reading of the Masoretic Text.

Ruth 4:14

The single note for 4:14 is marked with the letter *a*. The variants are as follows:

MT   שְׁמוֹ

LXX   τὸ ὄνομά σου

Robinson suggests for the reading of the Septuagint a retroversion of שְׁמֵךְ. The Masoretic Text speaks of "his [the child's or Yahweh's] name" while the Septuagint speaks of "your [Naomi's] name." That 4:15 continues talking about the newborn child without a specific indication of a new subject tips the balance against the reading of the Septuagint.[87]

Ruth 4:15

Note *a* in 4:15 refers to an idiosyncrasy of the Leningrad Codex: אֲהֵבְתֶךְ instead of the expected reading אֲהֵבָתֶךְ, which is found in other printed editions of the Hebrew Bible and more than twenty medieval manuscripts. There is no difference in meaning.

Ruth 4:16

The Syriac omits the words bracketed by the letters *a–a*: וַתִּשְׁתֵהוּ בְחֵיקָהּ. There is a slight possibility for the copying error known as homoeoarkton:[88] the first word omitted (וַתִּשְׁתֵהוּ) has the same two initial consonants and vowels as the first word after the omission (וַתְּהִי). Thus the *Vorlage* of the Syriac might not have had these words due to this copying error. That the Septuagint agrees with the Masoretic Text confirms that the Masoretic Text is original.

Ruth 4:18

The single letter *a* (which is not repeated in 4:18) refers, therefore, to the entire verse—in fact, to 4:18–20. The note

---

87. See Campbell, *Ruth*, 163–64.
88. See the earlier discussion of this scribal error in chapter 6.

calls attention to and suggests a comparison with the close parallel of these verses in 1 Chronicles 2:5, 9–15.

Ruth 4:19

The letter *a* in 4:19 is repeated and in this case refers to both words. The variants are as follows:

MT	רָם
Alexandrinus, Vaticanus	Αρραν
other LXX witnesses	Αραμ

Robinson further suggests that the text should read אָרָם, which is similar to the form found in the New Testament reference to this individual: Ἀράμ in Matthew 1:3–4. The spelling of the name in 1 Chronicles 2:9–10 is identical to the spelling in the Masoretic Text of Ruth (i.e., רָם). The Septuagint of 1 Chronicles 2:9–10 adds more confusion by referring to both Ραμ (Ram) and Αραμ (Aram), the second name not corresponding to any Hebrew element in 2:9. And in 2:10 Αραμ is listed as the father of Amminadab. It appears that the Septuagint of 1 Chronicles may be a conflate text, representing both Ram and Aram as sons of Hezron. Given that the variable spelling of names is a rather common feature in the Old Testament, both in the Hebrew text and the versions, a possible solution is that these are simply variant forms of the name of a single individual.[89]

Ruth 4:20

Another case of variation in regard to personal names is found in 4:20:

MT	שַׂלְמָה

---

89. Further information can be obtained in Homer Heater, "A Textual Note on Luke 3.33," *Journal for the Study of the New Testament* 28 (1986): 25–29.

Vaticanus   Σαλμαν

other LXX witnesses   Σαλμων

The reading found in the New Testament is Σαλμών (Matt. 1:4–5). The majority reading of the Septuagint (Σαλμων) is probably an assimilation to the form of 4:21.

Ruth 4:21

The last problem indicated in the textual apparatus of *BHS* for the Book of Ruth is in 4:21. The problem is related to the previous textual note, for it refers to the same individual by a different form of that name. Whereas in 4:20 the Masoretic Text reads שַׂלְמָה, in 4:21 the Masoretic Text reads שַׂלְמוֹן. Three to ten medieval Jewish manuscripts read שַׂלְמָה in agreement with the form found in 4:20. Vaticanus reads Σαλμαν, while the rest of the witnesses to the Septuagint read in agreement with the Masoretic Text. The reading of the medieval manuscripts would seem to be an adjustment to the expected form of the name that was used in the preceding verse. If we accept the Masoretic Text as it stands, then we have explicit testimony that the name of this individual existed in at least two forms. And in fact the author of the Book of Ruth used both forms in two verses, one after the other. Perhaps this helps with the sorting out of the previous problems in regard to the spelling of the names. There can be no doubt that the last named individual in 4:20 is the same person who is first named in 4:21. Since this is clearly the case in regard to this individual, perhaps it is also the case with regard to Ram/Aram in Ruth 4:19 and 1 Chronicles 2:9–10.

Conclusion

With this the survey of the textual data of the Book of Ruth is complete. The primary purpose has been to gain exposure to the field of textual criticism in a short book of the Old Testament. The textual character of Ruth is not the same as every other Old Testament book, but at least it offers a selection of many kinds of textual errors. The following chapter will serve as a conclusion to the present book and will indicate how the interested reader can pursue further study of the Old Testament text.

Conclusion

In the preceding pages the reader has been introduced to the two primary areas within the field of Old Testament textual criticism—the history of the transmission of the Old Testament text (chaps. 2–4) and the principles and procedures that are required for determining which of several variant readings is the most probable wording of the original text (chaps. 5–8). Three things remain to be done. In the first place, some concluding remarks are in order based on the preceding chapters of this book. Second, some comments are directed to the reader who wants to continue with the work of textual criticism in the Old Testament. And finally, it will be useful to outline what the reader should do who wants to pursue more advanced work on the text of the Old Testament.

Concluding Remarks

The preceding pages have described something of the care with which the text of the Hebrew Bible has been transmitted through time. The composition of this book, even with the aid of a computer, has illustrated to me just how easy it is to err in writing and copying a text. It is important to remember the long time periods during which the Old Testament text was transmitted only by hand copying. It is also fitting to recall the historical ebb and flow of the nation of Israel, the receiver and guardian of the Old Testament text. When these are coupled with the nature of writing materials in antiquity and the climatic conditions in Palestine, it is amazing that we have any text of the Old Testament. And it is doubly amazing that we have an excellent copy of the text preserved in the Masoretic Text.[1] It is important to remember that the Old Testament text has been in continuous circulation since the time of its initial writing. Its text is far better attested than *any* other document of comparable age.

The chapter devoted to the textual commentary of the Book of Ruth illustrates something of the state of the Masoretic Text in a particular book of the Old Testament. In all of the textual problems addressed in the apparatus of *BHS*, only one resulted in the failure to determine a probable original reading.[2] Many of the textual problems cited were of minimal importance to exegesis, and the rest were of only minor import. While the specific results for the Book of Ruth cannot be applied across the board to the rest of the Old Testament, at least the results for this short book give the beginning student an overall appreciation for the state of the Masoretic Text.

Guidelines for Continued Work

This book is only an introduction for the intermediate Hebrew student. The reader by now has been exposed to the history of the transmission of the Old Testament text and to the principles and practice of Old Testament textual criticism. The reader now needs to apply what was learned to other books and sections of the Old Testament. The place to begin is with the apparatus of *BHS*, although the beginning exegete will also want to make a careful study of the Septuagint text that corresponds to the section of Masoretic Text being studied. The student or pastor will also want to use a variety of commentaries that discuss textual issues. Three series are especially important. The first, the International Critical Commentary, has been around for many years, but is still

1. I am aware that the quality of the text is not the same in all books of the Hebrew Bible. The Masoretic Text of Samuel–Kings is notorious for its difficulties. But the point being stressed here is the overall quality of the text.

2. See the discussion of Ruth 2:7 in the preceding chapter.

valuable. The second, the Anchor Bible, will give additional resources to the student. Finally, a newer series, the New International Commentary on the Old Testament, also offers information on textual matters. In addition, the beginning exegete will want to investigate individual commentaries for the Old Testament book being studied.

Hints for the Advanced Student

For those who want to specialize in the textual study of the Old Testament, there are at least three areas in which to invest time and energy. The first area for further study involves obtaining the skills necessary to work independently in the critical editions of the various ancient versions of the Old Testament. The necessity for this individual work in the ancient versions is based on the incomplete and occasionally inaccurate information in the critical apparatus of *BHS*.[3] These skills include the ability to read Greek, Aramaic, Syriac, and Latin. Most seminary graduates have a working knowledge of Hebrew and Greek, and those languages are the most important for Old Testament textual criticism. But the advanced student must be able to work in the critical texts of the Targums, the Peshitta, the Old Latin, and the Vulgate.[4] If this is more than available time will allow, at the very least one should make a careful comparative study of the Masoretic Text and the Septuagint for a given passage or book of the Old Testament.[5]

A second area of additional study for the advanced student should be the ability to read unpointed Hebrew. This will allow the student to make use of the information that can be obtained in the biblical scrolls found at Qumran, Masada, and elsewhere. In addition, the student should learn to read the script of the Samaritan Pentateuch so that the information available in this witness to the text of the Pentateuch can be

3. See the previous discussion of this point in the introduction.
4. The reader should refer to the various sections of chapter 3 where the availability of critical editions for the various versions is discussed.
5. Even a careful use of the Rahlfs's edition can indicate possible variants that are not indicated in the apparatus of *BHS*.

independently studied. The material to be "harvested" from this phase of work will supplement and, on occasion, correct data in the apparatus of *BHS*.

A final area of interest for advanced textual study relates to the new products derived from advances in computer technology that have recently become available for text-critical work. Two new tools should be mentioned in this regard, both under the supervision of the Septuagint Tools Project. The first is the parallel alignment project of the Hebrew and Septuagint texts.[6] To date, ten biblical books have been completed,[7] and preliminary results have been published.[8] Second is the morphological analysis of the Septuagint. This work will be used to create new concordances as well as to facilitate the study of word distribution, lexicography, and syntax in the Septuagint.[9] These two projects, and the tools that they will make available, should provide help for the advanced student who is interested in becoming involved in more detailed textual work in all parts of the Old Testament.

Finally, it is hoped that this book has laid an adequate foundation for the intermediate student in the field of Old Testament textual criticism. Because the Old Testament has been accepted as God's revelation by believing people of all ages, it is of primary importance that the reader knows what, in fact, God said in a particular passage. The aim of the textual criticism of the Old Testament is to enable the reader to hear—and thus be able to respond to—God's Word accurately in spite of the varied history and sometimes varied wording of the transmission of that written revelation through time.

6. See the descriptive article by John R. Abercrombie, "Computer Assisted Alignment of the Greek and Hebrew Biblical Texts—Programming Background," *Textus* 11 (1984): 125–39.

7. Ibid., 137.

8. Ibid., 126 and n. 3.

9. See the descriptive article by William Adler, "Computer Assisted Morphological Analysis of the Septuagint," *Textus* 11 (1984): 1–16.

Appendix:
An English Key to *BHS*

By special arrangement with the American Bible Society, this appendix reproduces with minor modifications the first portion of "An English Key to the Latin Words and Abbreviations and the Symbols of *Biblia Hebraica Stuttgartensia*" by Hans Peter Rüger. Symbols and versions are explicated in table 9 above; for other sigla, consult "Sigla et Compendia Apparatuum" in *BHS*, pages xliv–l.

Abbreviations for Canonical and Deuterocanonical Books of the Bible

Gn	Jes	Zeph	Est	——	Ph	2P
Ex	Jer	Hag	Da	Mt	Kol	1J
Lv	Ez	Sach	Esr	Mc	1Th	2J
Nu	Hos	Mal	Neh	Lc	2Th	3J
Dt	Jo	Ps	1Ch	J	1T	Jd
Jos	Am	Hi	2Ch	Act	2T	Apc
Jdc	Ob	Prv	——	Rm	Tt	
1S	Jon	Ru	Est apkr	1Ko	Phm	
2S	Mi	Cant	1Makk	2Ko	Hbr	
1R	Na	Qoh	Sir	G	Jc	
2R	Hab	Thr	Jub	E	1P	

Latin abbrev. or word	English meaning	Sample location
a, ab	from	Nu 32:32c
abbreviatio, -onis	abbreviation	Jos 15:49a
abbreviatum	abbreviated	Ex 36:8b
aberratio oculi	visual error	Nu 9:23a-a
abhinc	hence	Ex 36:8b
abiit	he has departed	2Ch 21:20b-b
abs (absolutus)	absolute	Nu 8:12a
abstractum, -i	abstract	Jer 7:32a
absumuntur	they are ruined	Ps 37:20a-a
abundantia	abundance	Ps 72:16a
abundavit	he has abounded	Jes 57:9a
ac	and, and besides; to	Lv 16:10a; 2S 10:6b
acc (accentus, -us)	accent	Gn 35:22a-a
acc (accusativus)	accusative	Lv 27:31a
accusavit	he has accused	Jes 41:27b
act (activum)	active	Ex 31:15a
acuta, -ae	acute, accented	Lv 18:28a
ad	to	Gn 4:7b-b
add (additum)	added	Gn 2:19c-c
adde	add	Nu 24:24g-g
addit	it adds	Neh 9:10a
additamentum, -i	addition	2Ch 12:11a
addunt	they add	Jos 22:34b
adjunget	it will join	Jer 33:13a-a
admodem	very	Ex 36:8b
adverbialis	adverbial	Da 11:7c
aeg (aegyptiacus, -a, -um; -e)	(in) Egyptian	Jos 15:9a-a
aeneus, -a, -um	brazen	1Ch 18:8g
aequalitas	equality	Ez 48:2–7a-a
aequavit	he has compared	Jer 48:6b
aes	copper, bronze	Jdc 5:14d
aeth (aethiopicus, -a, -um; -e)	(in) Ethiopic	1S 19:20b
aeva	generations	Ps 90:5a
afflictans, -antis	vexing	Jer 46:16e
agnus	lamb	Jes 5:17d
agri, -orum	fields	Jer 39:10a
akk (akkadicus, -a, -um; -e)	(in) Akkadian	Jos 13:3a
al (alius, -a, -um; -ii, -ae, -a)	other(s)	Gn 32:18a
alias	elsewhere	2R 14:29a

Latin abbrev. or word	English meaning	Sample location
alibi	elsewhere	2S 2:7b
aliena	another's, foreign	Lv 18:21b
aliqui	some	Lv 18:11a
aliquot	some	2S 17:8b
alit (aliter)	otherwise	Ex 4:25a-a
altare, -is	altar	Jos 22:34b
alter, -a, -um	another, the other	Hi 16:20a-a
alterutrum	either, one of two	1R 5:14b
altus	high	Jes 11:11a
amicus	friend	Jes 44:28a
amplius	more	Ex 20:19a-a
an	or	Ez 1:8b-b
angeli, -orum	angels	Ps 89:7a
angulus, -i	angle, corner	Ez 8:3c
anhelare	to pant	Dt 33:21a
animadversio	attention	Hi 4:20a
animalia	animals	Ps 50:11b
annus	year	Nu 20:1a
ante	before	Gn 49:26a-a
antea	before this	Jdc 2:16a
aperiens	opening	Ex 13:13a
aperte	openly	Ps 12:6d-d
apertio	opening	Hab 2:3a
apertus	open	Nu 24:3b
apud	at, with	Jdc 20:27a-a
aquae, -arum	waters	Jer 51:12a-a
aquosi	abounding in water	Jer 31:40d
arab (arabicus, -a, -um; -e)	(in) Arabic	Nu 16:1a
aram (aramaicus, -a, -um; -e)	(in) Aramaic	Gn 15:2a-a
aranea	cobweb	Ps 90:9d
arbor, -oris	tree	Jes 44:4a
art (articulus)	article	Est 2:14a
ascensus, -us	ascent	2Ch 9:4c
asseritur	it is delivered	Jer 25:14c
assimilatum	assimilated	Da 4:14b
ast (asteriscus, -i)	asterisk	Dt 4:21e
at	but	Da 2:5a

Latin abbrev. or word	English meaning	Sample location
Atbaš	a device in which a word is spelled by substitution of the last letter of the alphabet for the first, the next to last for the second, etc.; hence the name alep-taw-bet-šin	Jer 25:25a
attulit	he has brought	Jes 61:6a
auctus	augmented	Hab 3:2a
aucupes	fowlers	Jer 5:26a-a
audacia	courage	Da 3:29a
auster, -tri	south	Ps 107:3c
aut; aut . . . aut	or; either . . . or	Nu 15:28a; 15:29a
auxiliator	helper	Ps 62:8b
aversio, -onis	turning away	Jer 31:19a
aves, -ium	birds	Dt 14:12a
bab (babylonicus, -a, -um)	Babylonian	Jes 52:14c
bellator	warrior	Ex 15:3b
bene	well	2Ch 4:2a-a
benedixit	he has blessed	1R 5:15c
bestia	beast	Hos 9:13a-a
bis	twice	Ex 6:2a
bonum	good	2Ch 3:6a
boves	oxen, bulls	1Ch 18:8g
brachium	arm	Jes 63:5c
brevis	short	Hi 8:14b
brevius	shorter	Dt 29:14a
c (cum)	with	Gn 1:11a-a
campus, -i	field	Jer 31:40d
canticum	song	Da 3:23a
capella	Capella (astronomy)	Am 5:9d
capillus, -i	hair of the head	Jes 57:9b
captivitas	captivity	Thr 1:20a-a
castella	castles, citadels	2S 20:14a
castigatio	punishment	Hi 36:18b
catena, -ae	chain, fetters	Ps 66:11b
cave	beware of	Hi 36:18a
cecidit	it has fallen	Ps 55:5a
celeriter	quickly	Ex 12:21b-b

Latin abbrev. or word	English meaning	Sample location
celerius	quicker	Hi 4:19a
cet (ceteri, -ae, -a)	the others, the rest	1S 1:15a
cf (confer)	compare	Gn 1:6a
cj (conjunge, conjungit, conjungunt)	connect, it connects, they connect	Gn 1:11a-a
clandestina	hidden	2R 11:6b
clemens	merciful	Jes 9:16a
cod (codex)	codex, ancient manuscript	Gn 18:21a
codd (codices)	codexes, ancient manuscripts	Lv 18:11a
cogitare, cogitaverunt	to consider, they have considered	Hi 21:27a
collectivum	collective	Gn 40:10b
collocabit	he will place	Da 11:39a
commeatus, -us	provisions	Jes 61:6a
commutatum, commutavit	changed, it has exchanged	2Ch 25:23a-a
compl (complures)	several	Mal 2:15c
compone	arrange	Jer 40:1a
concretum	concrete	Jer 7:32a
confisus est	he has trusted in	Prv 18:10a
confusus, -a, -um	confused	Ex 36:8b
conjg (conjungendum)	to be connected	Neh 12:25b
conservatus, -i	preserved	Da 7:11a-a
consilia	counsels	Prv 31:3c
constituit	he has appointed	1Ch 26:1b
constructio	construction	Hi 31:11c-c
consuetudo, -inis	habit	2S 2:27a
contaminatum	contaminated	Jos 8:33c
contemptores	despisers, contemners	Sach 9:1c-c
contendo	I contend, I dispute	Hi 16:20a-a
contentio, -onis	contest, fight	Ps 55:19c
contextus, -us	context	Da 7:11a-a
continent	they contain	Prv 25:20a-a
continuantur, continuatur	they are joined, it is joined	Jer 19:2a-a
contra	against	Nu 31:16b-b
contrarium	contrary	Nu 12:1b-b
conventus, -us	meeting, assembly	Da 6:7a
conversatio, -onis	conversation	
cop (copula, -ae)	copula	Ex 1:1a
copiae, -arum	military forces	Da 11:6b
coram	in the presence of	Ps 18:41a-a

Latin abbrev. or word	English meaning	Sample location
cornu	horn	Ex 19:13a-a
corr (correctus, -a, -um)	corrected	2Ch 16:5a
correctio	correction	Hi 1:5a
corrigens	correcting	Ez 43:11d-d
corruptum	corrupt	1Ch 27:4b-b
cp (caput, -itis)	chapter	Gn 32:2a
crrp (corruptus, -a, -um)	corrupt	Ex 14:9a
crudeles	cruel	Nu 21:6a
cs (causa)	on account of	Jer 4:8a
cstr (constructus)	construct	Ps 75:7d
cum	when	Ex 19:13a-a
curat	he takes care of	Hi 20:20a-a
curculio	weevil	Jes 41:14a
cursus	running	Hi 4:20a
custodia	watch	Na 2:2c
custos, -odis	keeper, watcher	Ps 141:3a
dare, dat	to give, it gives	Dt 6:3d
de	from, by reason of	Nu 31:18a
dedisti	you have given	Ps 8:2a-a
deest	it is missing	Nu 13:7a-a
defatigare	to fatigue, to tire	Prv 6:3c
deficiens, -entis	missing	Esr 10:36a
deficient	they will fail	Da 12:4a
deformare	to deform	Prv 28:12b
deliciae, -arum	delight	Jer 6:2a-a
delirium	silliness	Ps 31:19a
deminutio	diminution, decrease	Hag 2:19a
deprecari	to deprecate, to pray against	Jes 47:11b
descendant	let them descend	Ps 31:18a
descriptio, -onis	description	Ez 40:7/8/9b
desiderare	to desire	Dt 33:21a
desideratus	missed	2Ch 21:20b-b
desiit	it left off, it ceased	Hos 7:16b-b
destinatus	destined	Hi 15:22a
desunt	they are missing	Ex 2:1a
detentus	detained	Ps 88:9b
detrahere	to take off	Neh 3:15d
deus	god	Ps 4:2b
dicteria, -iorum	witticisms	Hi 17:6a

Latin abbrev. or word	English meaning	Sample location
dies	day	Sach 1:1a
differt	it differs	Da 3:31a
dilecta	loved	Jer 49:4b
direxit	he has led	Jes 60:4a
distinctius	more distinctly	1Ch 10:7a
diu	a long while	Ps 35:15a
divinum	divine	Dt 33:27e
divisit	he has separated	Nu 16:1a
divulgavit	he has divulged	Hi 33:27a
dl (dele, delendus, -a, -um)	delete, to be deleted	Gn 1:11c
doce	teach	Ps 119:29a
doctrina, -ae	instruction	Prv 22:18a
domicilium	dwelling	1Ch 4:41b
domina, -ae	lady, mistress	Jer 31:22b-b
dominabuntur	they will rule	Ob 20a-a
dominus, -i	lord	Nu 31:16b-b
domus	house	Ps 46:5b
dttg (dittographice)	by dittography	Gn 20:4b-b
du (dualis)	dual	Dt 2:7c
dub (dubius, -a, -um)	doubtful	Nu 18:29b-b
ducis	*see* dux	
ducunt	they derive	Jer 44:10a
duodecies	twelve times	Jos 10:24e
dupl (duplex, -icis)	double	Gn 35:22a-a
dupl (duplum, -i)	doublet	Gn 18:6a
durus	hard	Jer 17:9a
dux, ducis	leader	1Ch 27:4b-b
dysenteria	dysentery	Mi 6:14c
e, ex	out of, from	Gn 16:11a
ea, eae	*see* is, ea, id	
eadem	*see* idem	
ecce	behold	Ex 17:16a
egerunt, egit	they have acted, he has acted	Nu 16:1a
egredientur	they will march out	Nu 24:24a
eiciendum	to be dislocated	Prv 22:17b-b
elationes	elevations	Hi 36:29b
electi, -orum	chosen	Nu 31:5a
elige	choose	Ps 37:37b
emendatus	emended	Sach 5:6a-a
emissarius	emissary	Jes 39:1b

Latin abbrev. or word	English meaning	Sample location
emphaticum	emphatic	Hi 11:11a
en	behold	Ex 2:9a
encliticum	enclitic	Jdc 3:2b
energicus, -a, -um	energic	Jdc 5:26a
eques, -itis	rider	Ps 33:17a
equi	horses	Sach 6:6a-a
erasum	erased	2S 10:16a
erat	it was	Nu 27:11d
erimus	we will be	Ps 20:8b
error, -oris	error	Hi 4:18a
es, esse, est	you are, to be, he, she, it is	
et; et . . . et	and; both . . . and	Gn 1:6a; Jer 43:13a-a
etc	et cetera, and so forth	Lv 1:7a-a
etiam	also	Dt 30:16c
etsi	although	1Ch 28:7a-a
euphemismus	euphemism	Hi 1:5a
ex	*see* e, ex	
exaltati	raised	Ps 56:3c-c
exarescere	to dry up	Hi 5:3a
exaudivisti	you have heard	Ps 38:16a-a
exc (exciderunt, excidisse, excidit)	they have dropped out, to have dropped out, it has dropped out	Ex 2:25a
excepto	except	Dt 14:12a
excipit	it continues	Hos 2:19a
excitantes, excitaverunt	causing, they have caused	Ps 140:3b
exegesis, -eos	exegesis	Dt 32:1a
exemplum, -i	example	1S 15:4a
exercitus	army	2R 25:11b
explicitum	explained	2S 13:39a
expone	make known	Nu 25:4c
exstat	it exists	Ex 36:8b
exsultare	to exult	Hi 31:29a
extendere	to extend, to stretch out	Ps 68:32c-c
extr (extraordinarius, -a, -um)	extraordinary	Gn 16:5a
f (femininus, -a, -um)	feminine	Gn 38:2a
facilior	easier	Jos 11:2a
false	falsely	Jos 1:1c
falso	falsely	Nu 25:8a-a

Latin abbrev. or word	English meaning	Sample location
falsum	false	Jer 21:13d
fecit	he has made	Ps 105:20a-a
fem (femininus, -a, -um)	feminine	Jes 49:15a
fere	nearly, almost	Jos 16:10a
fides	loyalty	Ps 17:15b
fiducia	trust, confidence	Ps 84:6c
filius, -ii	son	1Ch 7:15c
fin (finis, -is)	end	Ex 36:8b
finire	to end	Hi 27:8a
finit (finitum)	finite	Jes 46:1a
firmus	firm, strong	Jes 44:12c
flagitium	crime	Ps 36:2b-b
fluvius, -ii	river	Hi 20:28b
follis	pair of bellows	Prv 26:21a
fontes	sources	Hi 28:11a-a
forma	form	Gn 16:11a
fortis, -e	strong	Ps 20:8b
fortitudo	strength	Nu 23:22c
fossa	ditch, trench	Da 9:25c
fovea, -ae	pit	Ps 17:14e
fragmentum	fragment	Sach 7:7a
franges	you will break	Ps 18:41a-a
frater, -tris	brother	Hi 20:20a-a
fremitus	roaring	Hi 4:14a
frequentavit	he has frequented	Jes 44:9b
frt (fortasse)	perhaps	Gn 1:21a
fugiant	they flee	Ps 60:6c
fui, fuit	I have been, he has been	Da 10:13a-a
fulge	shine forth	Ps 35:3a
furor	fury, rage	Ps 81:16b
gemma	jewel	Prv 26:8b
generatim	generally	Nu 7:19a–23a
genitor, -oris	begetter, father	1Ch 8:7b
genus	kind	Jes 40:20a
gl (glossa)	gloss	Gn 4:7b-b
gladius, -ii	sword	Ps 17:13a
gloria, -ae	glory	Ps 8:3a
glossator	glossator	Jer 48:6b
graece	(in) Greek	1Ch 27:33a

Latin abbrev. or word	English meaning	Sample location
hab (habent, -et)	they have, they esteem; it has	Ex 20:17a
habita	inhabit, live	Ps 11:1b
habitaculum, -i	dwelling	Ps 46:5b
hae, haec	*see* hic, haec, hoc	
hasta, -ae	spear, lance	Ps 35:3a
hebr (hebraicus, -a, -um; -e)	(in) Hebrew	Dt 17:9a-a
hemist (hemistichus)	hemistich	Jes 9:5c
hic	here	Gn 4:8a
hic, haec, hoc; hi, hae, haec	this; these	Ps 147:8a
hinc	hence	Hos 5:15b
hoc	*see* hic, haec, hoc	
homark	homoeoarkton	Gn 31:18a-a
homines	men	Nu 24:17h
homtel	homoeoteleuton	Lv 1:8b-b
honor	honor	Prv 5:9b
hora, -ae	hour	Esr 9:4b-b
hostes	enemies	Ps 9:7b
hpgr (haplographice)	by haplography	Gn 41:31a
hpleg	hapax legomenon	Jdc 3:23a
huc	hither	Gn 1:6a
humilis	simple	Hi 12:18a
iam	already	Dt 33:2c
ibi	there	2Ch 5:10b
ibidem	in the same place	Jer 39:8a
id	*see* is, ea, id	
id (idem)	the same	Nu 1:9a
idem, eadem, idem	the same	1R 8:16b
ignis	fire	Hi 18:15a-a
ii	*see* is, ea, id	
imbres	showers of rain	Na 1:12a-a
immergite	immerse	Jer 51:12a-a
imp (imperativus)	imperative	Dt 2:4b-b
impar	unequal	2S 17:8b
imperia	empires	Ps 47:10c
impetus	assault, attack	Jes 14:31b
impf (imperfectum)	imperfect	1S 2:28a
improbabiliter	improbably	2S 18:14b
impudice	shamelessly	Nu 16:1a
in	in, into	Gn 20:16b-b

Latin abbrev. or word	English meaning	Sample location
inc (incertus, -a, -um)	uncertain, doubtful	Lv 21:4a
incendere	to set fire to	Nu 21:14b
incip (incipit, -iunt)	it begins, they begin	Gn 32:2a
incolae	inhabitants	1Ch 2:55a
increpatio	rebuke	Ps 30:6a
inde	thence	Da 3:31a
index	proof	Jer 29:24a-a
inf (infinitivus)	infinitive	Lv 14:43c
infirmitas	infirmity, weakness	Mi 6:14c
infodi	I have dug in	Neh 13:25b
iniquus	unjust	Ps 36:2b-b
init (initium)	beginning	Nu 17:2/3e-e
iniuste	unjustly	Nu 31:16b-b
ins (insere, -erit)	insert, it inserts	Gn 1:7a-a
inscriptio, -onis	inscription	Ps 119:130a
inserti, -orum	inserted	Jer 39:13a
insolite	unusually	Da 4:27a
intenta	intended	Ez 48:2–7a-a
inter	between, among	Nu 22:5c
interpretatio	interpretation	Jer 46:2a
interrogativum	interrogative	Dt 20:19b
interv (intervallum)	interval	Gn 4:8a
intransitivum	intransitive	Da 9:1a
introducens, -entis	introductory	Da 3:23a
inundationes	inundations	Na 1:12a-a
inusitatum	unusual	Da 1:2a
invenies	you will find	Ex 36:8b
invers, inverso ordine	in inverse order	Gn 19:28a-a
inverte	invert	Ps 34:16a
ipsi	themselves	Jer 15:11b
ira, -ae	anger, wrath	Ps 7:14a
irrepsit	it crept into	Da 9:3a
irritator	he who irritates	Ps 15:4b
is, ea, id; ii, eae, ea	he, she, it; they	Jer 51:12a-a
it (item)	likewise	Ex 3:8c
iter	way	Jes 60:4a
iterum	again	Da 6:2a
iudicium	judgment	Hi 19:29a
iuravi	I have taken an oath	2Ch 7:18a
iustificata	justified	Gn 20:16b-b
iuvenes, -um	young men	Da 3:23a

Latin abbrev. or word	English meaning	Sample location
jdaram (judaeo-aramaicus, -a, -um)	Jewish-Aramaic	Da 4:12a
judaicus, -a, -um	Jewish	Jer 46:2a
judices	judges	Ex 21:6a
kopt (kopticus, -a, -um; -e)	(in) Coptic	Jes 19:10a
l (lege, legendum)	read, to be read	Gn 1:11b
laceravi	I have torn to pieces	Hi 19:20b
lacuna	lacuna	Ex 18:11a
laetantur	they rejoice	Ps 126:1b
lamentationes, -um	lamentations	Jes 43:14c
lapsus; lapsus calami	error; slip of the pen (scribal error)	Ex 23:3a
laquei, -orum	snares, traps	Ps 35:7b-b
largum	plentiful	Prv 13:23a
latitudo	breadth, width	2Ch 3:4a
lect (lectio)	reading	Gn 18:22a-a
lector, -oris	reader	Jer 2:31a-a
leg (legere, -it, -unt)	to read, it reads, they read	Nu 28:7b
legatur	let it be read	1Ch 27:27b
legiones	legions	Nu 24:24a
legisse, legit	to have read, it has read	Jer 5:24c
liber, -bri	book	Da 1:1a
libera	free (adj.)	Jer 34:5b
libera	release, free (verb)	Ps 12:8b
libere	freely	Dt 5:6a
licet	it is permitted	Ex 19:13b
lignum, -i	wood	Jes 40:20a
locus, -i	place	Nu 13:7a-a
locusta	locust	Jes 51:6a-a
longitudo, -inis	length	2Ch 6:13b-b
luna crescens	new moon	Jes 14:12a
luxa	put out of joint	Nu 25:4c
m (masculinum)	masculine	Nu 34:6c
magi	magicians	Jes 2:6a
magnificus	magnificent	Ex 15:11a
maiestas	majesty	Nu 23:21d
maj (major, -oris)	larger	Gn 34:31a
male	badly	Da 4:19a

Latin abbrev. or word	English meaning	Sample location
maledicta	abused	Jer 31:22b-b
malum	evil	Ps 10:6/7a-a
mandatum	order	Ps 17:4b
mansuetus	mild, gentle	Jo 4:11c-c
manus, -us	hand	Ps 68:32c-c
marg (marginalis)	marginal	2S 11:1a
marg (margine)	in the margin	Lv 25:22a
margo, -inis	margin	Hi 9:6a
masculum	male	Ex 13:13a
mavis	you prefer	Prv 13:4a
m cs (metri causa)	on account of the meter	Dt 32:9c
me	me	Jer 31:19a
mediator	mediator, intercessor	Hi 16:20a-a
meditatur	he thinks upon	Ps 10:6/7a-a
melior	better	1R 7:18d-d
melius	better	Dt 32:18b
mendacium, -ii	lie	Ps 139:24a
mendax	lying	Ps 15:3a
mendosus	incorrect	Esr 1:11a-a
mensa, -ae	table	2S 9:11c
mensis, -is	month	Jos 5:10b
meritum	reward	Ps 119:56a
Messias, -ae	Messiah	Nu 24:17e
metatheticum	postpositive	Jos 10:24e
metropolis, -eos	capital	Nu 22:39b-b
metrum	meter	Na 3:17b-b
meus, -a, -um	my	Jer 31:19a
min (minor)	smaller	Gn 2:25a
ministerium	service	Ps 26:8b
ministraverunt	they have worshiped	Ex 32:35a
misit	he has sent	1R 5:15c
mixtus, -a, -um	mixed	Ez 9:8b
mlt (multi, -ae, -a)	many	Gn 2:18a
momordi	I have bitten	Hi 19:20b
mors, -tis	death	Jer 11:19b
morus	mulberry tree	Jes 40:20a
mtr (metrum, -i)	meter	Ez 31:5a-a
mugire	to low, to bellow	Jer 31:39d
mulier	wife, woman	Lv 18:21b
munus	gift, bribe	1R 13:33b-b
murus	wall	Ps 122:3c

Latin abbrev. or word	English meaning	Sample location
mutanda, -atum, -atur	to be changed, changed, it is changed	Esr 1:9b
mutilatus, -a, -um	mutilated	Mi 1:10a
nab (nabataeus, -a, -um; -e)	(in) Nabatean	Dt 33:3a-a
Nabataeenses	Nabatean	Da 4:13a
narratum	told	1R 11:19a-a
navis	ship	Jes 2:16a
ne	lest	Ps 60:6c
necavi	I have slain	Neh 13:25a
nectunt	they weave	Jer 5:26a-a
nefarii	nefarious, impious	Ps 119:23a
neglecto	without regard to	Da 3:17a
neohb (neohebraicus, -a, -um)	modern Hebrew	Hi 18:3a
nequaquam	not at all	Da 9:13a
neutrum	neuter	Hi 31:11a
niger	black	Hi 3:5a
nil	nothing	Jer 5:24c
nisi	unless, but	Jer 5:24c
nobiles	highborn, superior	Jes 43:14a
noluerit	he is unwilling	1Ch 28:7a-a
nom (nomen, -inis)	name	Jos 15:25a
non	not	Ex 23:5a-a
nona, -ae	ninth	Esr 9:4b-b
nonn (nonnulli, -ae, -a)	some, several	Gn 1:30a
nostrum	our	Esr 4:14a
nota	note	2S 11:1a
notum	known	Hi 33:27a
novum	new	Ps 115:12a
nubes	cloud(s)	Nu 23:10c-c
nullus, -ius	not any	Hi 10:22b-b
num	(interrogative particle)	Ex 2:25a
numerus, -i	number	Ex 36:8b
nunc	now	Hi 9:6a
nuntius, -ii	messenger	Nu 22:18a
ob (obelus, -i)	obelus	Dt 4:22a
obducti, -orum	covered	Ps 68:31b
obiectum	object	Hi 17:6a
oblitus est	he has forgotten	Jes 44:9a

Latin abbrev. or word	English meaning	Sample location
obscure	darkly	Ex 23:5a-a
observatio	observation	Qoh 3:17a
obsistere	to resist, to oppose	Hi 38:11a-a
obturare	to block up	Hi 18:3a
offerebat	he brought before	1R 13:33b-b
om (omittit, -unt)	it omits, they omit	Gn 10:4a
omisso	with omission of	Est 9:29a-a
omnis, -e	all, every	Hi 10:8a-a
operati sunt	they have worked	Ps 73:7b
operuerunt	they have covered	Ps 55:5a
oppositum	opposite	Da 4:5a
oratio, -onis	prayer	Da 3:23a
ordinant, -at	they arrange, it arranges	Ex 20:13a
ordo, -inis	order	Nu 36:11a
orig (originalis)	original	Gn 18:22a-a
orig (originaliter)	originally	Gn 4:7b-b
ortus, -a, -um	arisen	Ez 40:14a
paenituit me	I have repented	Jer 31:19a
paenultima, -ae	the penultimate (syllable)	Lv 18:28a
papyrus, -i	papyrus	Da 3:6c
par (parallelismus, -i)	parallelism	Dt 33:13b
pars, -tis	part	Ps 35:3a
particula, -ae	particle	1S 2:27a
partim	partly, in part	Ex 36:8b
partitivum	partitive	Da 11:7b-b
pascuum, -i	pasture	Jer 6:2a-a
pass (passivum)	passive	Gn 45:2a
passim	here and there	Jer 2:33b
patronymicum	patronymic	Nu 13:7a-a
paululum	a little bit, trifle	Jes 57:17b
paulum	a little, somewhat	Jer 49:34a
pavor	fear	Ps 55:5a
pc (pauci, -ae, -a)	a few	Gn 1:11b
pellis, -is	skin, hide	Neh 3:15d
perdiderunt	they have destroyed	Ps 35:12a
perduces	you will bring through	Ps 49:20a
perfectus	perfect	Hi 10:8a-a
periphrasis, -eos	circumlocution	Ex 14:20a-a
permlt (permulti, -ae, -a)	very many	1S 2:10c

Latin abbrev. or word	English meaning	Sample location
pertinens, pertinet	belonging to, it belongs to	Neh 13:28a
perturbatus, -i	disturbed, disordered	Dt 26:17a
pessum data	destroyed	Na 3:11b
petent	they will ask, they will desire	Ps 18:42b-b
pf (perfectum)	perfect	Lv 18:28a
phoneticum	phonetic	Hi 36:27b
pinguis	fat	Hi 33:25a
pl (pluralis)	plural	Gn 13:18a
plaga	blow, stroke	Ps 39:11a
plerumque	generally	Dt 31:16c
plur (plures, -a)	many	Jos 19:47c
poetica	poetical	Hi 37:12c
populus, -i	people	Jer 33:13a-a
porta	gate	Da 8:2c-c
possessio	possession	Hi 15:29a
post	after	Gn 14:1d-d
postea	thereafter	Gn 47:5a
postquam	after	Cant 4:6a
potens, -entis	mighty	Dt 32:15f
potius	rather, preferably	Gn 48:20b
pr (praemitte, -mittendum, -mittit, -mittunt)	put before, to be put before, it puts before, they put before	Gn 1:30a
praebent, praebet	they present, it presents	Ex 36:8b
praecedens	preceding	Mal 2:15c
praecones	heralds	Ex 36:6a-a
praedicabit	he will praise	Ps 22:9a
praepos (praepositio, -onis)	preposition	2S 3:27c
praeter	except	Nu 22:22c
praeterea	besides	Ex 29:20a
prb (probabiliter)	probably	Jer 2:16b
primogenitum	first-born	Ex 13:13a
primus, -a, -um	first	1Ch 7:15c
princeps, -ipis	chief	Nu 24:17e
pro	for, instead of	Gn 11:31c
probavit	he has tested, he has tried	Jes 66:16b
proclamaverunt	they have cried out	Ex 36:6a-a
procurrens	jutting out	Hi 39:8a
pron (pronomen)	pronoun	1S 1:17a
propago, -inis	shoot	Ps 80:16a

Latin abbrev. or word	English meaning	Sample location
proprius, -a, -um	proper	Ex 2:1a
propter	because of	Nu 5:26b-b
propterea	therefore	Da 7:15a-a
prosperitas, -atis	prosperity	Hi 20:20a-a
protectio, -onis	protection	Ps 42:5a-a
prp (propositum)	it has been proposed	Jes 26:11a
prs (personalis, -e)	personal	1S 1:17a
pt (participium)	participle	1S 14:26a
pudicitia, -ae	decency	Nu 31:18a
pulchra	beautiful	Nu 12:1a
pulvis, -eris	dust	Nu 23:10c-c
pun (punicus, -a, -um)	Punic	Da 7:17a
punct (punctum, -i)	point(s)	Gn 16:5a
purus	pure	Prv 26:28b
quae	*see* qui, quae, quod	
quam	than	Hi 4:19a
quamvis	although	Dt 29:4c-c
quasi	as if, just as	Jer 5:26a-a
quattuor	four	Ez 5:12a
qui, quae, quod; qui, quae, quae	who, which	Nu 13:7a-a
quoad	as to, as far as	1Ch 27:4b-b
quocum	with whom	Hi 16:20a-a
quod	*see* qui, quae, quod	
quoties	how often	Hi 7:4b
radius	beam, ray	Jer 23:5b
rasura	erasure	Ex 36:29b
rebellaverunt	they have rebelled	Nu 31:16b-b
recte	correctly	Gn 31:46a
rectius	more correctly	Jer 4:20a
rectus, -a, -um	correct	Ez 32:6a
redii	I have returned	Da 4:33d
redime	redeem	Ps 12:8b
regalis	royal, regal	Hi 12:18a
regens	transitive; subject	Ez 43:7a; Hi 31:18a
regis	*see* rex	
regulariter	regularly	Da 5:27a
rel (reliqui, -ae, -a)	remaining	Jdc 14:2d
relat (relativum)	relative	1S 14:21a
reliquum, -i	rest	Jes 9:6a

Latin abbrev. or word	English meaning	Sample location
removeris	you have removed	Ps 22:2b-b
repens	creeping	Jer 46:22a-a
repetitus, -a, -um	repeated	Nu 25:8a-a
res, rerum	things	Gn 20:16b-b
restare	to stand firm	Prv 11:7f
rete	net	Jer 5:26a-a
retento	retained	Jer 18:14b
rex, regis	king	Jos 15:9a-a
robur	strength	Jes 54:8a
Romani, -orum	Romans	Nu 24:24b-b
rufi	reddish	Sach 6:6a-a
rursus	again	Jer 31:19a
saepe	often	Ex 21:28b
saepius	more often	Jos 10:24e
saginati	fattened	Ps 37:20a-a
sagitta, -ae	arrow	Ps 64:4a
sagittarius	archer	Prv 26:10b
sal	salt	Esr 4:14a
salus, -utis	salvation	Ps 22:2b-b
sam (samaritanus, -a, -um)	Samaritan	Jos 17:7b
sanctificate	sanctify, make holy	2Ch 35:3b
satiabor	I will be sated	Ps 16:11a
satiatus	sated	Hi 10:15a
saxetum, -i	rocky area	Nu 20:19a
saxum	rock	Hi 39:8a
scandendum	to be read aloud	Jo 2:9a
sciatis	you know	Hi 19:29a
scil (scilicet)	namely	Gn 27:40a
scribendum	to be written	Prv 22:17b-b
scriptor, -oris	writer, scribe	Hi 26:12a
se	himself, itself	Jer 33:13a-a
sec (secundum)	according to	Jer 4:20a
secundus, -a, -um	second	Ez 8:3d-d
sed	but	Gn 22:14a
semel	once, a single time	Jos 2:1e
semper	always	Gn 13:18a
senior	elder	1S 19:20b
sensus, -us	meaning	Jer 10:5a-a
sententia	opinion	Jes 44:28a
septies	seven times	Jos 2:1e

Latin abbrev. or word	English meaning	Sample location
sepulchrum	sepulcher, grave	Jes 53:9c
sepultura	burial	2Ch 26:23b
sequitur	it follows	2Ch 25:23a-a
sera	bar (for fastening doors)	1Ch 12:16b
serpens	snake	Jer 46:22a-a
seu	or	Gn 38:29a
sexta, -ae	sixth	2S 24:15b-b
sg (singularis)	singular	Gn 7:13a
si	if	Ex 23:5a-a
sic	so, thus	Gn 2:18a
silex	flint	Jer 18:14b
sim (similis, -e)	similar	Gn 11:11a
simillima	very similar	1Ch 28:20b
sine	without	Gn 26:1a
sive	or	Ex 16:32b
sol (solum)	only	Nu 16:24a-a
solus	alone, only	Dt 32:50b
sordes	dirt, filth	Prv 10:20b
soror	sister	1Ch 2:25b
sors	lot	Prv 12:9a
sperabunt, sperate	they will hope, hope	Ps 52:8b-b
spes, -ei	hope	Ps 55:23a
splendor, -oris	splendor, brilliance	Jer 23:5b
sq (sequens)	following	Ex 8:12c
sqq (sequentes)	following	Nu 3:12b
stat (status)	state	1S 12:23b
statim	immediately	Hi 18:8a
stella crinita	comet	Nu 24:17e
stercilinium	dunghill	Na 1:14c-c
stich (stichus)	stich	Jdc 5:11c
stillare	to drop, to drip	Hi 36:27a-a
stropha	strophe	Na 1:4b
studium	zeal	Prv 19:2b
sub	under, beneath	Ex 36:8b
subj (subjectum)	subject	1S 20:33b
subsellia	seats	2Ch 9:11a
subst (substantivum)	substantive, noun	2S 19:43b
suff (suffixum)	suffix	Gn 7:13a
sum	I am	Ps 88:9b
sumite	take	Ex 12:21b-b
summarium, -ii	summary	Da 5:25a

Latin abbrev. or word	English meaning	Sample location
sunt	they are	Mi 1:10a
super	above	Ps 56:3c-c
superesse	to be left	Na 3:14b
supervacaneus	needless, superfluous	Da 10:13a-a
supra	above	Jes 54:13a
suspensum	raised	Jdc 18:30a
suus, -a, -um	his	Ps 33:17a
syr (syriacus, -a, -um; -e)	(in) Syriac	Jer 10:5a-a
tacuerit, tacui	it was silent, I have been silent	Ex 19:13a-a
talpa	mole	Ps 58:9b
tantum	only	Nu 8:16a-a
tarditas	tardiness, slowness	Prv 29:11a
taurus	Taurus (astronomy)	Am 5:9c
te	you	Ps 16:2/3b-b
technicus	technical	Ez 41:6c
tegere	to cover	Hi 23:9a
tegimen	covering, cover	Na 2:4a-a
tegmentum, -i	covering, cover	Hi 23:9a
templum, -i	temple	2Ch 7:9a
ter	thrice	Jo 1:15a
terminus	term	Ez 41:6c
terra	land	Nu 22:5c
tertius, -ii	third	Ez 40:7/8/9b
testiculati	having their testicles	Jer 5:8b
testis, -is	witness	Lv 18:11a
tetragrammaton	tetragrammaton	2S 2:27a
textor	weaver	Jes 19:10a
textus, -us	text	Mi 5:4b-b
threnus, -i	lamentation	Ez 32:18c
tibi	to you	Dt 6:3d
titulus	title	Prv 22:17b-b
tonitrus	thunder	Jes 33:3a
tot (totus, -a, -um)	the whole	Dt 9:1a
tr (transpone)	transpose	Gn 1:6a
tradit	it renders, translates	Dt 5:6a
traditio	tradition	Jes 52:14c
transcendere	to transcend	Hi 39:8a
transcriptio, -onis	transcription, transliteration	2Ch 22:1a
transl (translatio)	translation	Hab 3:2a

Latin abbrev. or word	English meaning	Sample location
tu	you	Gn 20:16b-b
tum	then, in that case	Lv 17:4d-d
tumultuati sunt	they have made a tumult	Da 6:16b
tumultuose	tumultuously	Da 6:7a
tunc	then	Jo 2:9a
turma, -ae	division	1Ch 27:4b-b
tuus, -a, -um	your	Ps 17:15b
txt (textus)	text	Dt 33:2c
ubi	where	Esr 8:16c-c
ubique	everywhere	Nu 2:6a
ug (ugariticus, -a, -um; -e)	(in) Ugaritic	Dt 1:44b
ulciscendo	taking vengeance	Hos 9:12a
ultima	last	Nu 36:11a
ululatus	howling, wailing	Jer 4:31b
umbra, -ae	shadow	Ps 31:21c
una c (una cum)	together with	1R 9:16a
unde	wherefore	Ez 28:13c-c
unus, -a, -um	one	Da 11:7b-b
urbs, urbis	town, city	Jer 39:3b-b
urentes	burning	Nu 21:6a
usque ad	(right) up to	Ex 36:8b
ut	as; so that	Gn 6:20b; Hi 19:29a
uter, -tris	leather bottle	Ps 33:7a
utrumque	both, each	Na 1:10/11c-c
v (versus, -us)	verse	Lv 24:4a
vadum, -i	ford	Nu 21:11a
valde	very much	Da 3:31a
vallis	valley	Ps 84:7b
var (varia; varia lectio)	variant; variant reading	1R 7:18d-d
vasa	vessels	Hi 21:24a
vb (verbum, -i; verba, -orum)	word(s)	Ex 2:25a
vel	or	Gn 1:1a
venenum	poison	Jer 11:19b
venerunt, veniet	they have come, it will come	Da 6:7a
verb (verbum)	verb	1S 1:6a
verba	words	Lv 10:18a
verbatim	literally	Jos 16:10a

Latin abbrev. or word	English meaning	Sample location
verberatio	chastisement	Hi 36:18b
verbotenus	literally	Nu 10:11a
vere	verily, indeed	Hi 6:13a
veritas, -atis	truth	Ps 7:12a
vers (versio, -onis)	version, translation	Esr 2:48a
versus, -uum	verses	Jer 19:2a-a
vertit	it translates	Dt 8:13a
vertunt	they translate, they change	Nu 12:1b-b; Jer 5:10b-b
vestimenta, -orum	garments	Da 3:21a-a
vestis	garment	2R 23:7b
vetus	old	Nu 28:7b
vexant	they torment	Hi 6:4a
via	way	Ps 2:11/12c
vid (videntur, -etur)	they seem, it seems	Gn 10:4b
vide, videns	see, seeing	Jer 38:28a; Hi 10:15a
vindemiator	Vindemiator (astronomy)	Am 5:9e
vindex	liberator	Ps 4:2b
vinum	wine	Nu 28:7b
vita, -ae	life	Ps 143:10c
vivum	alive	2Ch 33:11a
vix	hardly, scarcely	Hos 6:5d
vobis	to you	Ex 19:13b
vocales	vowels	1Ch 11:22b
vocativus	vocative	Ps 113:1a
vos	yourselves	2Ch 35:3b
vox	word	2S 8:7b
vrb (verbum)	verb	Jdc 5:14a
vulva, -ae	womb	Ex 13:13a
vv (versus, -uum)	verses	1R 2:46a

Glossary

Aquila—early second-century A.D. reviser of the Septuagint known for his literal renderings

daughter translation—translation of an ancient text made on the basis of a prior translation of the original text; e.g., the Old Latin was made from the Septuagint, not from the Hebrew

dittography—scribal error resulting from the repetition of a letter(s) or a word(s)

Egyptian text family—group of Hebrew texts and versions that share significant similarities; the Septuagint and some Hebrew manuscripts from Qumran share many of these features

haplography—scribal error resulting from accidental omission of a letter(s) or a word(s)

Hexapla—six-column work of Origen; contained the Hebrew text, Greek transliteration of the Hebrew, the revisions of Aquila, Symmachus, and Theodotion, as well as Origen's own revision of the Septuagint

homoeoarkton—scribal error leading to omission of elements of the text that is based on similar beginnings of words

homoeoteleuton—scribal error leading to omission of elements of the text that is based on similar endings of words

***kaige* recension**—early revision of the Septuagint that aimed at conformity to the proto–Masoretic Text; also called proto-Theodotion

Kethiv—"that which is written"; text variant represented by the consonants that are written/printed in the text

local text—text type whose similarities are explained according to a hypothesized common geographic origin

Masorah *finalis*—"final Masorah"; Masoretic notations printed at the end of each Old Testament book

Masorah *magna*—"large Masorah"; register in *Biblia Hebraica Stuttgartensia* keyed to Masoretic notations in a separately published volume

Masorah *parva*—"small Masorah"; Masoretic notations printed in the outside margins of modern texts

Masoretes—Jewish scholars who devised a graphic system to represent the traditional vocalization of the Hebrew text

Masoretic Text—the standard Hebrew text of the Old Testament as transmitted by the Masoretes

Old Latin—earliest Latin version of the Old Testament; made from the Septuagint

Palestinian text family—group of Hebrew texts and versions that share significant similarities; the Samaritan Pentateuch shares many of these features

pesher—as used in context of Qumran, a commentary on an Old Testament book

Peshitta—the earliest translation of the Old Testament in Syriac

proto-Lucian—early revision of the Septuagint that aimed at agreement with the Palestinian text family

proto–Masoretic Text—text family with greatest representation in the biblical manuscripts at Qumran; very similar to the consonantal text later preserved by the Masoretes

Qere—"that which is read"; text variant represented by the vowels printed in the text and the consonants printed in the margin

recension—consciously made revision of an ancient text or translation; should be contrasted with a text type or family that develops naturally over time due to scribal errors

Samaritan Pentateuch—edition of the Torah preserved in archaic Hebrew script by the Samaritan community; allied with the Palestinian text family

Septuagint—Greek translation of the Old Testament (named for the traditional seventy translators) and its many revisions and recensions

Symmachus—late second-century a.d. reviser of the Septuagint characterized by good Greek style

Syro-Hexapla—translation of the fifth column of the Hexapla by Paul of Tella; contains the symbols Origen used to show differences between the Septuagint and the Hebrew text of his day

Targums—translation of the Old Testament in Aramaic; originally orally based, they are characterized by paraphrase

text type—group of texts and/or translations that share a significant number of common features

Theodotion—second-century a.d. reviser of the Greek text who made use of the *kaige* recension

transposition—scribal error resulting from a change in order of letters or words

variant reading—any reading in a Hebrew manuscript or version that disagrees with the accepted base text

Select Bibliography

Albright, William F. *The Proto-Sinaitic Inscriptions and Their Decipherment.* Harvard Theological Studies 22. Cambridge: Harvard University Press, 1966.

Barr, James. *Comparative Philology and the Text of the Old Testament.* Reprinted Winona Lake, Ind.: Eisenbrauns, 1987.

———."Review of *Biblia Hebraica Stuttgartensia*, edited by Karl Elliger and Wilhelm Rudolph." *Journal of Semitic Studies* 25 (1980): 98–105.

———. *The Typology of Literalism in Ancient Biblical Translations.* Mitteilungen des Septuaginta-Unternehmens 15. Göttingen: Vandenhoeck & Ruprecht, 1979.

———. *The Variable Spellings of the Hebrew Bible.* Schweich Lectures of the British Academy 1986. Oxford: Oxford University Press for the British Academy, 1989.

Barthélemy, Dominique. *Critique Textuelle de l'Ancien Testament.* 2 vols. to date. Orbis Biblicus et Orientalis 50. Göttingen: Vandenhoeck & Ruprecht, 1982–.

Barthélemy, Dominique, Alexander R. Hulst, Norbert Lohfink, William D. McHardy, Hans P. Rüger, and James A. Sanders. *Preliminary and Interim Report on the Hebrew Old Testament Text Project.* 5 vols. New York: United Bible Societies, 1979–80.

Biblia Sacra iuxta Latinam Vulgatam Versionem. 17 vols. to date. Rome: Polyglottis Vaticanus, 1926–.

Brooke, Alan E., Norman McLean, and Henry St. John Thackeray (eds.). *The Old Testament in Greek.* 3 vols. Cambridge: Cambridge University Press, 1906–40.

Burrows, Millar. *Burrows on the Dead Sea Scrolls* [combined reprint of *The Dead Sea Scrolls* and *More Light on the Dead Sea Scrolls*]. Grand Rapids: Baker, 1978.

Cross, Frank M. *The Ancient Library of Qumran and Modern Biblical Studies.* Revised edition. Reprinted Grand Rapids: Baker, 1980.

———. "The Contribution of the Qumran Discoveries to the Study of the Biblical Text." Pp. 278–92 in *Qumran and the History of the*

Biblical Text. Edited by Frank M. Cross and Shemaryahu Talmon. Cambridge: Harvard University Press, 1975.

————. "Early Alphabetic Scripts." Pp. 97–123 in *Symposia Celebrating the Seventy-fifth Anniversary of the Founding of the American Schools of Oriental Research (1900–1975).* Edited by Frank M. Cross. Cambridge, Mass.: American Schools of Oriental Research, 1979.

————. "The Evolution of a Theory of Local Texts." Pp. 306–20 in *Qumran and the History of the Biblical Text.* Edited by Frank M. Cross and Shemaryahu Talmon. Cambridge: Harvard University Press, 1975.

Cross, Frank M., Jr., and David N. Freedman. *Early Hebrew Orthography.* American Oriental Series 36. New Haven: American Oriental Society, 1952.

Díez Macho, Alejandro. "The Recently Discovered Palestinian Targum: Its Antiquity and Relationship with the Other Targums." Pp. 222–45 in *Congress Volume: Oxford, 1959.* Vetus Testamentum Supplement 7. Leiden: Brill, 1960.

———— (ed.). *Neophyti I: Targum Palestinense MS de la Biblioteca Vaticana.* 6 vols. Madrid: Consejo Superior de Investigaciones Científicas, 1968–79.

Driver, Godfrey R. "Abbreviations in the Massoretic Text." *Textus* 1 (1960): 112–31.

————. "Once Again Abbreviations." *Textus* 4 (1964): 76–94.

Dupont-Sommer, André. *The Essene Writings from Qumran.* Translated by Geza Vermes. Cleveland: World, 1962.

Elliger, Karl, and Wilhelm Rudolph (eds.). *Biblia Hebraica Stuttgartensia.* Stuttgart: Deutsche Bibelgesellschaft, 1977.

Fitzmyer, Joseph A. *The Dead Sea Scrolls: Major Publications and Tools for Study.* Revised edition. Society of Biblical Literature Resources for Biblical Study 20. Atlanta: Scholars Press, 1990.

Freedman, David N. "The Massoretic Text and the Qumran Scrolls: A Study in Orthography." Pp. 196–211 in *Qumran and the History of the Biblical Text.* Edited by Frank M. Cross and Shemaryahu Talmon. Cambridge: Harvard University Press, 1975.

Gall, August F. von (ed.). *Der hebräische Pentateuch der Samaritaner.* Giessen: Töpelmann, 1918. Reprinted 1966.

Ginsburg, Christian D. *Introduction to the Massoretico-Critical Edition of the Hebrew Bible.* London: Trinitarian Bible Society, 1897. Reprinted New York: Ktav, 1966.

Gordis, Robert. *The Biblical Text in the Making: A Study of the Kethib-Qere.* Second edition. New York: Ktav, 1971.

Goshen-Gottstein, Moshe H. "Hebrew Biblical Manuscripts." Pp. 42–89 in *Qumran and the History of the Biblical Text*. Edited by Frank M. Cross and Shemaryahu Talmon. Cambridge: Harvard University Press, 1975.

———. "The Rise of the Tiberian Bible Text." Pp. 666–709 in *The Canon and Masorah of the Hebrew Bible*. Edited by Sid Z. Leiman. New York: Ktav, 1974.

———. *Text and Language in Bible and Qumran*. Jerusalem: Orient Publishing, 1960.

———. "The Textual Criticism of the Old Testament: Rise, Decline, Rebirth." *Journal of Biblical Literature* 102 (1983): 365–99.

———. "Theory and Practice of Textual Criticism: The Text-Critical Use of the Septuagint." *Textus* 3 (1963): 130–58.

Greenberg, Moshe. "The Stabilization of the Text of the Hebrew Bible, Reviewed in the Light of the Biblical Manuscripts from the Judean Desert." *Journal of the American Oriental Society* 76 (1956): 157–67.

———. "The Use of the Ancient Versions for Interpreting the Hebrew Text." Pp. 131–48 in *Congress Volume: Göttingen 1977*. Vetus Testamentum Supplement 29. Leiden: Brill, 1978.

Jellicoe, Sidney. *The Septuagint and Modern Study*. Oxford: Clarendon, 1968.

——— (ed.). *Studies in the Septuagint: Origins, Recensions, and Interpretations*. New York: Ktav, 1974.

Kahle, Paul E. *The Cairo Geniza*. Second edition. Oxford: Blackwell, 1959.

Kenyon, Frederic. *Our Bible and the Ancient Manuscripts*. Fourth edition. New York: Harper, 1941.

Klein, Michael L. *The Fragment-Targums of the Pentateuch according to Their Extant Sources*. 2 vols. Analecta Biblica 76. Rome: Pontifical Biblical Institute Press, 1980.

Klein, Ralph W. *Textual Criticism of the Old Testament: From the Septuagint to Qumran*. Guides to Biblical Scholarship. Philadelphia: Fortress, 1974.

Leiman, Sid Z. (ed.). *The Canon and Masorah of the Hebrew Bible*. New York: Ktav, 1974.

McCarter, P. Kyle, Jr. *Textual Criticism: Recovering the Text of the Hebrew Bible*. Guides to Biblical Scholarship. Philadelphia: Fortress, 1986.

McCarthy, Carmel. *The Tiqqune Sopherim and Other Theological Corrections in the Masoretic Text of the Old Testament*. Orbis Biblicus et Orientalis 36. Göttingen: Vandenhoeck & Ruprecht, 1981.

McNamara, Martin. *Targum and Testament*. Grand Rapids: Eerdmans, 1972.

———. "Targums." Pp. 856–61 in *The Interpreter's Dictionary of the Bible: Supplementary Volume*. Edited by Keith Crim. Nashville: Abingdon, 1962.

Milik, Jozef T. *Ten Years of Discovery in the Wilderness of Judaea*. Translated by John Strugnell. Studies in Biblical Theology 26. London: SCM, 1959.

Millard, Alan R. " 'Scriptio Continua' in Early Hebrew: Ancient Practice or Modern Surmise?" *Journal of Semitic Studies* 15 (1970): 2–15.

O'Connell, Kevin G. "Greek Versions (Minor)." Pp. 377–81 in *The Interpreter's Dictionary of the Bible: Supplementary Volume*. Edited by Keith Crim. Nashville: Abingdon, 1962.

The Old Testament in Syriac according to the Peshitta Version. Edited by Pieter A. H. de Boer. Leiden: Brill, 1972–.

Purvis, James D. "Samaritan Pentateuch." Pp. 772–77 in *The Interpreter's Dictionary of the Bible: Supplementary Volume*. Edited by Keith Crim. Nashville: Abingdon, 1962.

———. *The Samaritan Pentateuch and the Origin of the Samaritan Sect*. Cambridge: Harvard University Press, 1968.

Rahlfs, Alfred (ed.). *Septuaginta*. Stuttgart: Württembergische Bibelanstalt, 1935.

Roberts, Bleddyn J. "The Old Testament: Manuscripts, Text and Versions." Pp. 1–26 in *The Cambridge History of the Bible*, vol. 2: *The West from the Fathers to the Reformation*. Edited by Geoffrey W. H. Lampe. Cambridge: Cambridge University Press, 1969.

———. *The Old Testament Text and Versions*. Cardiff: University of Wales Press, 1951.

———. "The Textual Transmission of the Old Testament." Pp. 1–30 in *Tradition and Interpretation*. Edited by George W. Anderson. Oxford: Clarendon, 1979.

Scott, William R. *A Simplified Guide to BHS*. Berkeley: BIBAL, 1987.

Silva, Moisés. "Review of *The Text-Critical Use of the Septuagint in Biblical Research*, by Emanuel Tov." *Westminster Theological Journal* 45 (1983): 423–26.

Skehan, Patrick W. "The Biblical Scrolls from Qumran and the Text of the Old Testament." Pp. 264–77 in *Qumran and the History of the Biblical Text*. Edited by Frank M. Cross and Shemaryahu Talmon. Cambridge: Harvard University Press, 1975.

Sperber, Alexander (ed.). *The Bible in Aramaic*. 4 vols. Leiden: Brill, 1959–73.

Stuart, Douglas. "Inerrancy and Textual Criticism." Pp. 97–117 in *Inerrancy and Common Sense*. Edited by Roger R. Nicole and J. Ramsey Michaels. Grand Rapids: Baker, 1980.

Talmon, Shemaryahu. "The Old Testament Text." Pp. 159–99 in *The Cambridge History of the Bible*, vol. 1: *From the Beginnings to Jerome*. Edited by Peter R. Ackroyd and Christopher F. Evans. Cambridge: Cambridge University Press, 1970.

―――. "The Textual Study of the Bible—A New Outlook." Pp. 321–400 in *Qumran and the History of the Biblical Text*. Edited by Frank M. Cross and Shemaryahu Talmon. Cambridge: Harvard University Press, 1975.

―――. "The Three Scrolls of the Law That Were Found in the Temple Court." *Textus* 2 (1962): 14–27.

Thomas, D. Winton. "The Textual Criticism of the Old Testament." Pp. 238–59 in *The Old Testament and Modern Study*. Edited by Harold H. Rowley. Oxford: Clarendon, 1951.

Tov, Emanuel. "Criteria for Evaluating Textual Readings: The Limitations of Textual Rules." *Harvard Theological Review* 75 (1982): 429–48.

―――. "A Modern Textual Outlook Based on the Qumran Scrolls." *Hebrew Union College Annual* 53 (1982): 11–27.

―――. "The Nature and Study of the Translation Technique of the LXX in the Past and Present." Pp. 337–59 in *Sixth Congress of the International Organization for Septuagint and Cognate Studies*. Edited by Claude E. Cox. Atlanta: Scholars Press, 1987.

―――. "The Orthography and Language of the Hebrew Scrolls Found at Qumran and the Origin of These Scrolls." *Textus* 13 (1986): 31–57.

―――. *The Text-Critical Use of the Septuagint in Biblical Research*. Jerusalem: Simor, 1981.

―――. *Textual Criticism of the Hebrew Bible*. Minneapolis: Fortress, 1992.

Ulrich, Eugene. "Horizons of Old Testament Textual Research at the Thirtieth Anniversary of Qumran Cave 4." *Catholic Biblical Quarterly* 46 (1984): 613–36.

Vaux, Roland de. *Archaeology and the Dead Sea Scrolls*. Revised edition. Schweich Lectures 1959. London: Oxford University Press, 1973.

Waltke, Bruce K. "Aims of OT Textual Criticism." *Westminster Theological Journal* 51 (1989): 93–108.

―――. "Samaritan Pentateuch." Vol. 5 / pp. 932–40 in *The Anchor Bible Dictionary*. Edited by David N. Freedman et al. Garden City, N.Y.: Doubleday, 1992.

———. "The Samaritan Pentateuch and the Text of the Old Testament." Pp. 212–39 in *New Perspectives on the Old Testament*. Edited by J. Barton Payne. Waco, Tex.: Word, 1970.

———. "The Textual Criticism of the Old Testament." Vol. 1 / pp. 211–28 in *The Expositor's Bible Commentary*. Edited by Frank E. Gaebelein. Grand Rapids: Zondervan, 1979.

Weber, Robert (ed.). *Biblia Sacra iuxta Vulgatam Versionem*. 2 vols. Third edition. Stuttgart: Württembergische Bibelanstalt, 1985.

Weingreen, Jacob. *Introduction to the Critical Study of the Text of the Hebrew Bible*. New York: Oxford University Press, 1982.

Wevers, John W. "Text History and Text Criticism of the Septuagint." Pp. 392–402 in *Congress Volume: Göttingen 1977*. Vetus Testamentum Supplement 29. Leiden: Brill, 1978.

Wiseman, Donald J. "Books in the Ancient Near East and in the Old Testament." Pp. 30–48 in *The Cambridge History of the Bible*, vol. 1: *From the Beginnings to Jerome*. Edited by Peter R. Ackroyd and Christopher F. Evans. London: Cambridge University Press, 1970.

Wonneberger, Reinhard. *Understanding BHS: A Manual for the Users of Biblia Hebraica Stuttgartensia*. Second edition. Translated by Dwight R. Daniels. Subsidia Biblica 8. Rome: Pontifical Biblical Institute Press, 1990.

Würthwein, Ernst. *The Text of the Old Testament*. Translated by Erroll F. Rhodes. Grand Rapids: Eerdmans, 1979.

Yeivin, Israel. *Introduction to the Tiberian Masorah*. Translated and edited by E. John Revell. Masoretic Studies 5. Missoula, Mont.: Scholars Press, 1980.

Subject Index

Author Index

Scripture Index